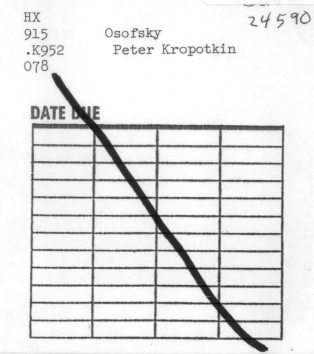

TWAYNE'S WORLD LEADERS SERIES

EDITOR OF THIS VOLUME

Arthur W. Brown
*University of Miami,
Coral Gables*

Peter Kropotkin

TWLS 77

Peter Kropotkin

PETER KROPOTKIN

By STEPHEN OSOFSKY
Hofstra University & New York University

TWAYNE PUBLISHERS
A DIVISION OF G. K. HALL & CO., BOSTON

Published in 1979 by Twayne Publishers,
A Division of G. K. Hall & Co.
All Rights Reserved

Printed on permanent/durable acid-free paper and bound
in the United States of America

First Printing

Library of Congress Cataloging in Publication Data

Osofsky, Stephen.
Peter Kropotkin.

(Twayne's world leader series; TWLS 77)
Bibliography: p. 193–98
Includes index.
1. Kropotkin, Petr Alekseevich, Kniaz', 1842-1921.
2. Anarchism and anarchists.
HX915.K952078   335'.83'0924 [B]   78-12051
ISBN 0-8057-7724-5

Dedication

This book is dedicated to my wife Diana for an incredible job of editing under the most difficult of circumstances and for a major contribution to the revision and reworking of the substantive content, and to my daughters Alexandra and Alys in hopes of a more Kropotkinian tomorrow for their generation; finally, I wish to acknowledge the help of my mother for her customary support and my in-laws for their extraordinary stints of baby-sitting, no small contribution to the completion of this effort.

Contents

About the Author

Stephen Osofsky was born on April 27, 1938, in Far Rockaway, New York. He received his B.A. from the University of Pennsylvania, M.A., Certificate of the Russian Institute and Ph.D, from Columbia University, and J.D. from the University of Michigan. He has taught at Muhlenberg College, Nassau Community College, The University of Tennessee, and New York University, where he was Visiting Associate Professor of Politics and is now Adjunct Associate Professor. He is presently on the faculty of the Hofstra University School of Business. Dr. Osofsky is the author of *Soviet Agricultural Policy—Toward the Abolition of Collective Farms* (Praeger Publishers, N.Y.: 1972), and has published some eight articles and numerous reviews in American and foreign journals.

Preface

The literature on Peter Kropotkin is not extensive and the best of it is primarily biographical rather than a study of his ideas and influence. Yet Kropotkin is the most impressive anarchist theoretician, and anarchist themes and values, particularly in their Kropotkinian variant, seem current and influential in present-day social criticism among a wide spectrum of schools. We have recently had a splendid biography of Kropotkin by Martin A. Miller, whose excellent doctoral dissertation traced his formative years. Miller's most recent work complements the earlier biography by George Woodcock and Ivan Avakumovic, which still retains great value. Miller's focus is less on the times and the movement and more on the individual and the complexities of his personal intellectual development.

I have placed Kropotkin within the anarchist tradition in Chapter 2 in order to provide an intellectual context for those primarily interested in Kropotkin's contribution to the development of anarchist thought and, in turn, its relation to Marxian thought. My biographical chapter (Chapter 1), in addition to conveying the basic factual data, seeks to survey the impact of his personality and thought on his contemporaries. Chapter 3 attempts to set forth the crucial components of Kropotkin's social theory while Chapter 4 subjects these views to a comprehensive critical analysis by the wide spectrum of political criticism from left to right, with the author's views emerging from the interplay of the various critical viewpoints and schools presented. Chapter 5 attempts to trace the intellectual heirs of Kropotkin both inside and outside the anarchist tradition and movement.

The purpose of this volume is to delve thoroughly and comprehensively into and sift out the essentials of Kropotkin's socioeconomic-political views, to gauge his contribution to anarchist theory and, beyond this, to modern political theory. I put forward the view that Kropotkin was and remains a very significant social critic who helped define today's social and political agenda. While the constraints of format and length required of an introductory study preclude an exhaustive analysis and critique of Kropotkin's theoretical points, I have been able to treat what I consider his crucial thoughts, hypotheses, and critiques without, I feel, neglecting knowingly any significant topic or dimension of his thought, and without thereby distorting, rendering superficial, or undermining whatever coherence his theory has. I feel that the unique contribution this book makes to the literature is precisely its elaboration and evaluation of Kropotkin's social thought both in the context of his times and ours. My interest has been primarily in the exposition and implications of Kropotkin's social theory on the enduring debate over the ends and meaning of social life rather than on Kropotkin the sectarian or the exemplar of a nineteenth-century Russian revolutionary.

Chronology

1842   Peter Kropotkin born in Old Equerries' Quarter of Moscow on December 9.

1846   In April, Peter, age three and one-half, and brother Alexander, not yet five, are left to care of nurses when mother, age thirty-five, dies of consumption.

1850   At a Royal Ball attended by the Tsar Nicholas I the eight-year-old Peter is singled out by the Tsar for his charming costume and immediately inscribed as a candidate for the Corps of Pages.

1857   Peter enters the Corps of Pages school in St. Petersburg, a privileged student body of 150 students, mostly children of the court nobility; the school combined the character of a military school and a court institution attached to the Imperial household; Peter and Alexander commence a regular correspondence which will extend to 1871.

1859   Peter begins to edit his first revolutionary paper, advocating the necessity for a constitution for Russia in the school underground.

1861   Peter nominated Sergeant of Corps of Pages as reward for being the top student in the upper form, a status that included being Page de Chambre of the Emperor and which placed Peter on certain occasions right in the midst of court life.

1862   Peter chooses his future service in the unfashionable Amur Cossacks; spends the next five years in Siberia.

1864   Alexander joins Peter in Irkutsk.

1866   Polish prisoners in Siberia rebel and are severely dealt with; both brothers decide to leave the military in disillusionment.

1867   Peter and Alexander settle in St. Petersburg, with Peter studying physics and mathematics at the university and Alexander studying in the military academy for jurisprudence.

1872   First trip to Western Europe; in Switzerland he is favorably impressed with the Jura Federation; soon after his return to Russia he joins the populist underground Chaikovsky Circle.

1874   Peter arrested by the Third Section, the secret police, for agitation and imprisoned in fortress of Peter and Paul; Alexander soon arrested.

1876   Peter's friends succeed in a plot to get him out of prison and he escapes to England via Scandinavia; journeys to Switzerland and joins the Jura Federation of the International Workingmen's Association.

1878   Marries Russian Jewish student refugee in Switzerland.

1879   Kropotkin and two friends start a revolutionary fortnightly paper in Geneva called *Le Revolté*.

1880   Jura Federation declares itself in favor of anarchist-communism.

1881   Following the assassination of Alexander II the Swiss government banishes Kropotkin.

1883   Kropotkin arrested and tried in Lyon in the wake of large-scale unemployment and labor unrest; transferred from Lyon to Clairvaux prison to serve a five-year sentence.

1885   Publication of *Paroles d'un Revolté*.

1886   Kropotkin released from prison and settles in England; soon starts an anarchist monthly in London called *Freedom*.

1887   Birth of Kropotkin's only child, Alexandra, and publication in England of *In Russian and French Prisons*.

1890   Publishes article "Mutual Aid among the Animals" in *The Nineteenth Century*, the first of a series on the subject which will ultimately be published together in book form as *Mutual Aid* in 1902.

1892   *La Conquete du Pain* published in Paris; only in 1906 is a complete English version published.

1897   First visit by Kropotkin to North America; meets Johan Most, Benjamin Tucker, and Emma Goldman; tries to see Alexander Berkman in jail but is rebuffed by the authorities.

1898   Memoirs published as *Memoirs of a Revolutionist* by the *Atlantic Monthly*.

1899   *Fields, Factories and Workshops* published in Boston by Houghton, Mifflin & Co.

1901 Second trip to U.S. Invited by Lowell Institute of Boston to lecture on Russian literature. These lectures published in book form in 1905 as *Ideals and Realities in Russian Literature.*

1905 Comes out in favor of dropping the French anarchists' anticonscription line for the sake of strengthening France against the threat of German militarism.

1909 Publication of *The Great French Revolution* in both French and English. Published in Russian only after the February revolution in 1917; *The Terror in Russia* published in England.

1912 Kropotkin's seventieth birthday celebrated in London and Paris with meetings.

1913 *Modern Science and Anarchism.*

1914 Kropotkin's defense of England and France on the outbreak of the war splits the anarchist movement. Lenin brands Kropotkin and the Marxist Plekhanov "chauvinists" for their defensist position.

1917 On June 12, Kropotkin arrives in Petrograd and refuses Provisional Government's offer of a portfolio made personally by Prince Lvov; in August he addresses National State Conference and equates the defense of Russia with the defense of the revolution.

1918 Kept in political isolation by the Bolshevik regime in Dmitrov, forty miles from Moscow. Refuses to associate himself with the Bolshevik regime.

1919 Emma Goldman visits the Kropotkins in Dmitrov; in May Kropotkin meets Lenin in Moscow to protest the Bolshevik hostage policy.

1920 Writes letters to Lenin protesting the woes caused to localities by Bolshevik centralization of authority and the hostage system; writes letter to Western workers asking them to induce their governments to stop their intervention in Russia while condemning the Bolshevik dictatorship.

1921 February 8, Kropotkin dies of pneumonia; Bolsheviks allow the Kropotkin house in Moscow to be set up as a Kropotkin museum.

1938 Kropotkin Museum closed down.

CHAPTER 1

A Most Useful Life

THE "Arnarchist Prince" Peter Kropotkin, was born in 1842 in Moscow, in a mansion in the old aristocratic quarter. His father, an almost Gogolesque petty nobleman, ruled by a military mentality typical of his class which owed nothing to the possibly exhilarating experience of combat, had an estate of some 2,000 souls—adult males exclusive of women. These subjects he ruled with an arbitrariness and petty vindictiveness mitigated only by his incompetence.

From such roots came the superfluous young men of Tsarist Russia, the Fathers and Sons, the Oblomovs and the Onegins. But unlike Bazarov or Pechorin, Peter Kropotkin overcame the sloth and comfortable aimlessness which was his birthright. He forsook a snug sinecure in the Tsarist military and civil service as well as the much-deserved status of Secretary of the Imperial Russian Geographical Society in order to live a life of use to humanity, a vision which compelled him to forsake the very promising scientific career in geology-geography (begun as an intellectually ravenous youth of twenty) during his five-year military service as a Cossack officer in East Siberia. He had, in fact, during his Siberian experience, insured his place in the annals of geography by discovering a major error in the geographical descriptions of the East Siberian mountain ranges. Soon thereafter he would win additional academic laurels by formulating his hypotheses about the glaciation of Scandinavia and Northern Russia and his theory about the existence of a large island north of Novaia Zemlia which, it turned out, was confirmed although the official discovery was to be credited to an Austrian expedition some time later because of the failure of the Tsarist government to appropriate funds for the expedition proposed by Kropotkin.

Despite his manifest scientific talents and the great sense of

17

satisfaction he derived from his scientific work, he chose to devote himself to service for the people. This decision, seen from the perspective of his time and personal circumstances, meant the forfeiture of his scientific career and all his security. This was not a sudden decision, however. His intellectual and emotional development, especially as revealed by his famous correspondence with his elder brother Alexander (1857–1871), pointed toward such a decision although not without revealing some formidable cross pulls. As of sometime in 1872, he had become a revolutionary in mind if not in action.

His revolutionary career was spent mainly behind the desk and the podium rather than the barricades. It ended in a distinctly backwater town, Dmitrov, some forty miles north of Moscow, on a note of quiet futility in physical enfeeblement and great spiritual discouragement, and was set against an almost total political isolation from the course of the revolution he had waited for so long and so sorely wished to serve. His funeral provided the by then vanquished Russian anarchist movement with an officially condoned and controlled occasion to vent their esteem for this last great personal link to that which was purest and most free in the great Russian revolutionary tradition. They were honoring the Kropotkin whose great revolutionary works were written well before 1914.

The Kropotkin who returned to Russia in 1917 had compromised himself among most anarchists by supporting the Western powers in the First World War. He had compounded this offense against anarchism's antiwar principle by insisting on his return to Russia that the Russian people would support the war. His position did much to undermine his prestige among socialists of all stripes and badly split the anarchist movement. But even those most bitterly disappointed did not question his integrity. And his actions in attempting to intercede on behalf of arrested anarchists during the period 1917–1921 as well as for all political hostages, coupled with his staunch defense of the Russian revolution and an unequivocal antiinterventionist position, somewhat recouped his lost luster. Still, in the last analysis, he had totally failed to leave any imprint on the Russian revolution. Fortunately his tactical errors, if such they were, and the ravages of old age could not efface his intellectual labors of previous decades.

Kropotkin's influence over subsequent generations of diverse intellectuals is hardly the measure of his coherence as a theoretician, but it does suggest the universal quality of his appeal. Such diverse literary figures as the Chinese novelist Pa Chin and James Joyce, the Irish master, were heavily influenced by Kropotkin. Pa Chin, a favorite of the leftist Chinese students of the 1930s, was a devotee of Kropotkin's ideas and translated many of his major works into Chinese.[1] And according to James Joyce's most eminent interpreter, Richard Ellmann, Kropotkin was a major influence on Joyce's political views.[2]

Kropotkin's measure as both a theoretician within the anarchist tradition and a social theorist is attested to by critics of various political persuasions. To Bertrand Russell, Kropotkin's works constitute the nearest approach to a finished and systematic body of anarchist doctrine.[3] According to Richard Drinnon, the biographer of Emma Goldman, it was with Kropotkin that anarchism came to its fullest and finest theoretical expression.[4] G. D. H. Cole pronounced Kropotkin to have been unquestionably the leading figure in the development of anarchist-communism as a social doctrine.[5] For James W. Hulse, he was Europe's leading theoretical anarchist.[6] According to E. H. Hobsbawn, with the exception of Kropotkin, it is not easy to think of an anarchist theorist who could be read with real interest by nonanarchists,[7] a view shared by Robert Nisbet.[8] Martin A. Miller feels that Kropotkin was, after Bakunin's death in 1876, unquestionably the most widely read and respected anarchist theorist.[9] Roger N. Baldwin credits him with being the first man to formulate a scientific basis for the principle of anarchism.[10] Paul Avrich sees Kropotkin as the foremost libertarian theorist and most venerated figure of the anarchist movement.[11] In Alexander Gray's opinion, Kropotkin "is probably the most representative, as he is certainly the most attractive and engaging, of the modern anarchists."[12] For Gerald Runkle, Kropotkin "with his scholarly and saintly ways ... almost brought respectability to the movement."[13]

Kropotkin was the most widely read of all the anarchist propagandists, with his books and pamphlets translated into the major Eastern as well as European languages:

> They appealed to guerilla fighters like Makhno in the Ukraine and Zapata in Mexico, as well as to reformers like Ebenezer Howard and Patrick Geddes. His inventive and pragmatic outlook made him for George Orwell one of the most persuasive of anarchist writers.[14]

Richard Hare pays Kropotkin a mixed compliment which

seems to ring true as an accurate description of his intellectual and emotional powers:

> For Kropotkin's lucid scientific mind made the unattainable earthly Paradise sound more plausible, without becoming less attractive. His unworldly, almost saintly character, generous conduct, and brave adventurous life, distracted attention from his extreme political naivete. He created an indelible impression, especially in France and England, on humane scientists, members of the liberal professions and skilled artisans. . . .[15]

Kropotkin's anarchist colleagues and friends provide some rather interesting evaluations of the man and his work. On one thing they and virtually all other observers agree: his moral character and integrity are of the highest order. Typical of the evaluations of nonanarchist acquaintances are those of James Mavor and Henry Hyndman, who knew Kropotkin in England during his long years of exile there. Hyndman, as a Marxist, was an ideological adversary who was impressed by the charm of Kropotkin's manner and the unaffected sincerity of his tone. Despite their rather intense arguments, Hyndman felt that Kropotkin was not an opportunist.[16] Mavor, a fellow geographer and a friend, pays Kropotkin homage by calling him a moral genius. He was less interested in politics or economics than in the moral attitudes of men. But, unlike Tolstoi, Kropotkin "reconciled the practical conduct of life with his ideas; and he did so in a manner which inflicted no obligation upon anyone else."[17]

Max Nomad, a student of revolutionaries, considered Kropotkin a stainless hero among those few revolutionaries untouched by greed for power or riches. He was a revolutionary humanitarian rather than a practical revolutionist.[18] Kropotkin's longtime friend and fellow revolutionary, Sergei Stepniak, although not of the anarchist persuasion, reflects the consensus that Kropotkin was a thinker rather than a man of action. He notes that Kropotkin was a great speaker, moving because of his obvious sincerity. Kropotkin was often willing to admit his position was incorrect.[19]

The Danish literary critic and friend of Kropotkin, Georg Brandes, echoes Mavor and Hyndman in his compliments. "He does not impose sacrifices upon others. He makes them himself. This man is modesty personified."[20]

The view of anarchist activist and chronicler Rudolf Rocker

reinforces the positive picture of Kropotkin's character: "There was no cleavage between the man and his world. He spoke and acted in all things as he felt and believed and wrote. Kropotkin was a whole man."[21]

The anarchist writer and historian Nicholas K. Lededev portrays Kropotkin as a lover of humanity, of real people, not merely man in the abstract. He feels that Kropotkin had much in common with Tolstoi, who very much wanted to meet Kropotkin. But unlike Tolstoi, Kropotkin was a lover of life, not a renouncer of earthly things.[22] According to V. Chertkov, a close friend of Tolstoi's, the passionate pacifist and Christian anarchist was impressed with Kropotkin's justification of the use of force. He was also very much taken with Kropotkin's *Memoir of a Revolutionist.*[23]

S. Ianovski relates that Kropotkin all his life avoided meetings with reporters. He did not want "to be copy."[24] Henry S. Salt, a British friend of Kropotkin, describes an incident revealing of Kropotkin's love for his fellow man:

We met a troop of beggers who were decidedly professionals. Kropotkin responded to their appeal. The second time that day on being approached, he responded. Kropotkin's reply to the obvious question was: "Yes, I know they are probably imposters and will drink the money at the public house; but we are going back to our comfortable tea, and I cannot run the risk of refusing help where it may possibly be needed."[25]

Catherine Breskovskaia comments that "he is admired as a prophet whose every word was in accord with his pure life."[26] And Paul Reclus, the brother of Elisee Reclus, a confidant of Kropotkin's, sums up his character thusly: "Kropotkin's main characteristic was ... his kindness. It overflowed from his eyes, enveloped one, warmed one instantly."[27] For Errico Malatesta, Kropotkin's contemporary and a leading anarchist figure, Kropotkin was "... the most greatly humane man I have ever known in my life."[28] Will Durant testifies to the impression made on him by a visit to Kropotkin: "I parted from him as I used in early days to go out from church—tense and awed with a sense of something whole and priceless in the experience. I have never met a finer man."[29]

For the anarchist Anna Goldman, Kropotkin was her "great teacher" and was recognized by friend and foe as one of the greatest minds and most unique personalities of the nineteenth century.[30]

There is some difference of opinion—perhaps more a matter of degree—over just how willing Kropotkin was to change his position in the face of a better argument. I have already mentioned Stepniak's testimony to the effect that Kropotkin was open to criticism. Jean Grave, a close friend of Kropotkin's and an anarchist writer, wrote that Kropotkin "...knew how to surrender to an argument when it struck him as sound."[31] Kropotkin, who was utterly reticent about his personal life, had a heated argument with Emma Goldman when Emma intensely disagreed with Kropotkin's criticism that too much space in certain of her writings was devoted to sexual questions. In Kropotkin's view, woman's equality was not a sexual but a mental question. When women are equal intellectually and share man's social ideals, they will be free, he argued. Emma's rejoinder was that when she reached his age, the sexual question would no longer seem of importance! Kropotkin, smiling and amused, granted that perhaps Emma was right.[32] Yet Errico Malatesta, who credits Kropotkin with having done more than Bakunin to elaborate and propagandize anarchist ideas, also says Kropotkin could not calmly suffer contradiction.[33]

What emerges from this collage of paeans, testimonials, and judgments is a picture of very probably the most impressive proponent of anarchism, a dedicated and formidable theoretician with an evident warmth and charm. He was a man possessed of a deep-set modesty, and not without a sense of humor, a man who clearly practiced what he preached and eschewed material comforts and worldly honors, not out of a sense of philosophical asceticism but rather because of a scrupulous regard for the revolutionary principles he wished to honor by personal example.

I   Childhood, Boyhood, and Youth

The Kropotkins were descended from the Grand Princes of Smolensk. Peter's father, Alexander, was a typical officer of the time of Nicholas I. He had serfs in three different provinces plus other large tracts cultivated by peasants. In their fashionable Moscow mansion there were fifty servants and half as many in the country home. According to Peter, his father never bought or sold serfs to or from strangers. And while he was likely to fall into fits of rage, he possessed a natural instinct toward leniency. Alexander liked to do everything outside the home in the grand manner but was rather niggardly in his approach to the family's daily needs. Kropotkin described his father as ruling despotically over his serfs and family—on the whole an illiterate, coarse, but honest man somewhat troubled by his rather barren military record.[34] His father was not a big drinker or boaster. His vice was card-playing, and there were occasions when he lost substantial sums. What deeply disturbed the young Peter most about his father were the episodes in which he ordered servants and serfs to be beaten. More commonly there were scoldings administered in front of the children which mortified Peter.[35]

Peter was one of the four children of Ekatarina Sulima, the daughter of General Nicholas Sulima, a hero of the 1812 war and later a governor-general of Western and Eastern Siberia. The Sulimas were descendants of a Zaporozhe cossack chieftain. Ekatarina was a warm, artistic soul revered by the servants. Nicholas, her oldest child, was born in 1834, then Helen in 1835, Alexander in 1841, and Peter in 1842. According to Peter: "She had the nature of an artist. . . . All who knew her loved her. The servants worshiped her memory."[36]

Ekaterina died of consumption in April 1846, at thirty-five, leaving Peter, three and one-half, and Alexander, not yet five. The elder brother, Nicholas, age twelve, and Helena, eleven, were not living at home. The father was seldom seen by the two young boys, their upbringing being left largely to their German nurse. Peter's love of the servants who cared for him so tenderly later grew into a strong compassion toward the serfs and peasants on the estate, whom he came to know intimately in many cases and who rekindled the image of his dearly beloved mother by telling the boys anecdotes about their kind mistress. Peter describes his debt to these simple folk in the wake of his mother's death:

> I do not know what would have become of us if we had not found in our house, among the serf servants, that atmosphere of love which children must have around them.[37]

Years after her death, Peter discovered his mother's diaries, in which verses of the forbidden Decembrist poet Ryleev as well as of Byron and Lamartine were written in her own hand.[38] Peter's later love of literature, especially the Romantics, and his pronounced youthful artistic inclinations, might very well derive from the impress of his mother's image conveyed to him by the servants' tales. Perhaps, as one student of Kropotkin put it, he inherited his mother's refined feelings and artistic tendencies.[39] In any case, Peter embraced her memory as a moral force in his life:

> Men passionately desire to live after death, but they often pass away without noticing the fact that the memory of a really good person always lives. It is impressed upon the next generation and it is transmitted again to the children. Is not that an immortaliy worth striving for?[40]

Two years after his mother's death his father remarried, largely in response to the pressure of the powerful General Timofieff, who wanted to marry off his wife's niece.[41] The stepmother, Elizabeth Koradino, an admiral's daughter, was a shrewish and vindictive woman extremely antagonistic toward Alexander and at best indifferent to the other children. She had one child, a girl, with Peter's father. Jealous of Peter's mother's memory, she cut off all ties to the Sulima family and got rid of the older servants who were repositories of the first wife's legend.[42]

The first fifteen years of Peter's life were spent partly in the Moscow house and partly on the family estate at Nikolskoye, in Kaluga Province, some 160 miles from Moscow.[43] Peter's oldest brother, Nicholas, does not seem to have played any role in his life. He distinguished himself in the Crimean War but later disappeared in disgrace from a monastery where he had been committed because of his dissolute life-style.[44] After his mother's death, his upbringing became largely a matter for his French tutor and his successor, a Russian university student. Both he and Alexander were subjected to the same regime.[45] They both developed a great love for literature, especially for Gogol and Pushkin.[46]

Their father had never considered other than a military career for his sons. At eight, Peter took part in Nicholas I's twenty-five-year celebration ball, where the cream of Moscow society was represented. The Tsar personally picked him out because of his costume and rewarded him by inscribing his name as a candidate for the exclusive Corps of Pages Military Academy, which supplied the personal attendants of the imperial family. As a result, in the fall of 1857 Peter was sent to the corps school in Petersburg. He soon became the outstanding student in the school. In 1861 he was made a sergeant-major and designated a Page de Chambre of Emperor Alexander II.[47]

At this time Alexander was sent to another corps school in Orel. The separation of the two brothers, who had grown so close to each other, was bridged by a lively and frequent correspondence which would continue for well over a decade. It constituted a rich source in gauging their intellectual and emotional development and their effect on one another. At the outset of their correspondence Peter, at fifteen, had already evolved certain tastes and inclinations. He had developed a populist view on the burning issue of the day, the emancipation of the serf. He was also in revolt against authority, personified by his father, whom he rejected for forcing him into a career he had not chosen. He nurtured a very deep psychological wound born of his father's unloving relationship toward himself and Alexander.[48] He also had sided with the servants inwardly in their conflicts with his father, finding in them the emotional succor he had been denied by this remote martinet.

Peter's first year in the corps school brought his rebellious nature to the fore. He became involved in a direct clash of wills with the assistant director, General Giradot, a Frenchman. Peter revolted against the petty persecutions, hazings, and bullyings of the older boys, often unofficially encouraged by Giradot.[49] In standing up to Giradot Peter showed a courage and devotion to principle which would distinguish his conduct for the rest of his life.

Despite the bitter regimen of the school, it was intellectually rigorous in many areas, especially the sciences. Peter developed an intense interest in science and astronomy and also read widely in both French and German.[50] Reading warded off boredom, and Peter was fortunate in that his sister Helen, married and living in Moscow, allowed him the use of her husband's library.[51] It was also at this time that he developed a great love for music, especially opera.[52]

Peter's intellectual horizons were widening. During his first year in the corps school he translated Voltaire's *Philosophical Dictionary* into Russian, as well as works of Lamartine.[53] At the end of 1858 he discovered Herzen. During the next year he considered himself a constitutionalist [54] and indulged in his first underground revolutionary work—editing a reformist news sheet which he carefully circulated in the military school.[55]

The correspondence between Peter and Alexander which commenced in 1857 was not their first intellectual collaboration. Peter at twelve and Alexander at fourteen had contributed stories and poems for a home-created journal called *Vremmenik*, modeled after the famous *Sovremmenik* of Chernyshevsky.[56] There are certain aspects of the correspondence which should be noted. First, for the period of 1857-1862 (Volume I), Alexander clearly emerged as the instigator of ideas. Or perhaps one might better say that Peter is reacting to the ideas of Alexander, and doing so in a distinctly defensive manner. Second, the main political issue reflected in the correspondence is that of the abolition of serfdom. There is the persistent search of Alexander for a philosophical basis by which to live. Alexander clearly thirsts after the true meaning of life while Peter is cast in the role of skeptic. As I. Smilga concedes, both brothers emerge from the correspondence as liberals, not revolutionaries, with Peter, however, far to the left of Alexander, a position he was to maintain thereafter.[57]

Peter's appraisal of his brother's intellectual influence at this time seems both accurate and characteristically generous and modest:

> He was very much in advance of me in his intellectual development, and urged me forward, raising new scientific and philosophical questions one after another, and advising me what to read or to study. ... To him I owe the best part of my development ... and he advised me to get a purpose in my life worth living for.[58]

Two books published in 1859 were to loom large in the intellectual development of the two brothers: Darwin's *On the Origins of Species* and Louis Buchner's *Force and Matter*.[59] At that time, Alexander would espouse the views of Kant and Hegel while Peter would prefer Voltaire. In a series of letters running from September 1857 through the spring of 1858, Peter rejected his brother's attempted proselytizing for his newly embraced Lutheran faith. In a letter to Alexander on September 18, 1857, Peter rejects Lutheranism and protests that he has no religion whatsoever. He favors Voltaire's views of religion.[60] In a letter of

April 27, 1858, Peter asks Alexander for proof of God's existence. Alexander's reply indicates exasperation with his brother's skepticism and taunts Peter with the standard question: "Who created everything?"[61]

On the great issues of the moment, the peasant question and constitutional reform, Alexander clearly stood to the right of Peter. Alexander argues that a constitutional system is good only in developed countries. Russia is only beginning to develop, and only when all classes are reasonably well educated will constitutional government be possible. Alexander agrees that the serf should receive the land, but he differs with Peter on the issue of who should bear the costs. Peter believes that the Tsar should compensate the landlord while Alexander feels strongly that compensation should come from the ex-serfs themselves.[62] Later Alexander will accept Peter's view.

In the summer of 1858, Alexander had suffered his first of many intellectual reversals: he confesses in an August letter that he is no longer a Lutheran. Christ, he feels, was only a man. He still insists that God is the creator, but feels the soul is mortal and there is no life after death. Alexander now essentially rejects Christian dogma.[63] Peter presses Alexander to admit that none of Christ's miracles or his resurrection can be proved.[64] From this time on, the religious question is transcended.

Alexander embraces the positivist materialism of Buchner and Moleshott. He urges Peter to accept his newly found view that thinking is a material process and that the natural sciences prove the absurdity of the idea of the soul. There is nothing except matter—"away with idealism."[65] But at this point the focus of their contention turns to careers.

Peter has already begun to think of a career. His father advises the Ministry of Foreign Affairs,[66] but Peter prefers a university education. Otherwise, he writes Alexander, he cannot be useful to members of society.[67] The need for a useful life becomes a leitmotif in Peter's correspondence.[68] In a letter of September 6, 1860, he asks Alexander what he would think of his going into a career in agriculture.[69] Peter's feeling of empathy toward the peasant was inclining him toward dedicating his life to the plight of the serf. All this was accentuated by the reform politics in the air, especially the much-discussed variants of the imminent emancipation.

Alexander, in contrast to Peter's enthusiasm for the promise of reform, seems to have retreated from the raging political questions to a privation born in part from frustration with his father's illiberal attitude toward his financial needs and from pessimism over the prospects of reform. He mentions in a letter of August 13, 1859, that he has often thought of suicide. His advice to Peter is to stress the physical sciences, not philosophy.[70] In a letter of February 10, 1861, he confesses: "I have no ideals: neither socialism nor communism do I believe in. I relate to social affairs as a critic. . . ."[71] Peter rejects his advice, which is to satisfy one's strongest needs in life. This, says Peter, is too easy. One must be a useful person.[72]

In 1861, Peter was nominated Sergeant of Corps of the Imperial Pages since he was the top student in the upper form of the school. As such he acted as the emperor's personal *page de chambre*,[73] a great honor and a tremendous recommendation for whatever career he would choose.[74]

Peter's tenure as *page de chambre* actually accentuated his discontent with the system and pushed him toward a more radical position. In 1861 he still considered Alexander II an admirable person, but, with the onset of an imperial policy of reaction, the repression of students riots in St. Petersburg, Poland, Moscow, and Kazan, and the discontinuance of Sunday schools set up to advance peasant literacy, he revised this opinion. The year as court page gave him a close-up of court life and he became utterly disillusioned. The venality of court administration perhaps accounts for the seeds of his deep distrust for government,[75] although it raised as yet no theoretical speculations.

II *The Siberian Years*

When Peter's tenure at the Corps de Pages ended in mid-1862, he had decided not to continue his career among the sycophants, intriguers, and job brokers of the palace political scene. Nor was the social life of the capital to his liking. Alexander, who had called it pure egoism when Peter talked of discharging his debt to society by seeking more education, now disapproved of his brother's tentative decision to seek a commission in the rather unfashionable Amur Cossacks. Peter's choice embodied three ambitions. By choosing a specialty in artillery, he could later study higher mathematics and chemistry and develop technical skills; he would be able to travel; finally, he could secure financial independence from his father.[76] Peter defended his decision, citing the region's healthier climate and the lower living expenses. The only negative aspect was that it meant not seeing Alexander. Peter explained that amidst nature he would feel and work better.[77] He later added in a letter confirming the finality of his decision that he looked forward to taking his leave in East Siberia and Japan.[78] Years later Peter explained that his decision to go to the Amur was in good measure in order to travel, to investigate and live close to nature, to meet strange tribes and to see polar and tropical vegetation, and the Tibetan tiger and the Yakutsk bear. He also felt that in Siberia there would be wider opportunities for socially useful work and for implementing the reforms which were being planned in St. Petersburg.[79]

His father opposed this seemingly perverse decision. But Peter overcame his father's attempt to block the move. In June of 1862 Peter left for Siberia.[80] He would remain in East Siberia for five years, returning to St. Petersburg in 1867 as a fully formed man with a definite world view.[81]

Peter's diary and letters record his youthful enthusiasm for the scenery and the peasants. He describes West Siberia as a rich and fertile land with each peasant cultivating twenty-five to forty desiatinas (1 desiatina equals 2.7 acres). The people are clever, gay, and look one straight in the eye.[82] These independent yeomen show a pride and a dignity of which the serfs of European Russia have been deprived. The implication is clear: a prosperous yeomanry could emerge in European Russia if the terms of emancipation were favorable. Peter also comments on the natural dignity of the aged Russian peasant women.[83] His compassion for the poor and aged is much in evidence in his diary.

Peter reported to M.S.Korsakov, the governor-general of East Siberia. Kropotkin was impressed with his openness to subordinates. Korsakov assigned him as an aide-de-camp to General Kukel, temporary governor-general of Transbaikalia, based in Chita.[84] Kukel was a liberal reformer of thirty-five, a brilliant Lithuanian who read Herzen's banned paper "The Bell"[85] and had been friendly with Bakunin—not yet an anarchist—while he was in Siberian exile. Peter wrote to Alexander on September 7, 1862:

The Governor of Trans-Baikal, Kukel, is a superior man according to everyone, young artistic, plays excellently, is a poet, and in general I find him very sympathetic, quiet, moderate, simple.[86]

Peter quoted Kukel's motto approvingly: "Any kind of force is nasty."[87] Peter wrote to Alexander on October 14, 1862, in forming him that he had spoken to Kukel about getting Alexander a post in East Siberia. Kukel thought he could probably do something.[88]

The Siberian experience proved rich for Peter. His disillusionment with the potential of reform from above became absolute. He indulged his youthful curiosity to the brim and engaged in geographical fieldwork which bore theoretical fruits. He also came into contact with exiled scientists who inspired him with their personal courage and their ideas. In Chita and Irkutsk he had no close friends. But part of the void was temporarily filled when he met two Decembrists in Chita, I. Zavaleshin and I. Gorbachevsky. Gorbachevsky was an ardent radical and absolute believer in "the people," and this affected Peter.[89].

Peter visited the exiled poet M. L. Mikhailov, who had been condemned to hard labor in 1861 for issuing a revolutionary proclamation. Unofficially, Kukel had treated Mikhailov very well, letting him live in his brother's home, where Peter visited him. Mikhailov advised Peter to read Proudhon's "System of Economic Contradictions." This was Peter's first contact with anarchist ideas. It made a great impression on him and stimulated his reformism. Peter still felt that great social questions could be resolved by peaceful means by organizing artels (work associations) financed by enlightened capitalists.[90]

Kukel involved Kropotkin in a series of reform projects. First there was a prison reform. Peter was impressed with the cruel and often inhuman prison conditions he met with on inspections. Another reform project was city self-government in East Siberia. His initial enthusiasm turned to cynicism when the central government indulged none of the proposed changes in December 1864.[91]

The Mikhailov "coddling," exposed by bureaucrats jealous of Kukel and threatened by his incorrigible integrity and the thrust of the prison and other reforms he so zealously championed, led to his dismissal in early 1863. There was also the factor of his refusal to take part in the suppression of the Poles. Kukel's fall was a great blow to Peter, and he reported the bad news to Alexander with a real sense of anguish.[92] Not even Peter's newfound interest in acting in Chita's theater productions[93] could distract him. Only his geographical expeditions invigorated him.[94] He escaped into a grand adventure which enlisted his newly acquired acting ability.[95] In 1864 he accepted a proposal that he make a geographical expedition into Manchuria, the object of which was to find a direct route across the triangular enclave of Chinese Manchurian territory which thrust up into Russian Siberia and elongated the route eastward from Chita to Vladivostok. The Chinese government was highly suspicious of Russian motives and so, disguised as a merchant, Peter commanded a group of cossacks on what was essentially a military reconnaissance expedition. Kropotkin devotes many pages to this great adventure in his "Memoirs."

When he returned from Manchuria, life in Chita in 1865 was epitomized by card-playing and time-serving.[96] Peter's appetite for geography and geology had been whetted by his interest in biology, already inspired by the luxuriant fauna and flora he had encountered in his travels. He became especially interested in the origin of species and their ability to survive but confessed to Alexander that he knew too little about biology.[97] In 1865, Peter explored the north slope of the East Siberian mountain chain and in 1866 he completed his most significant journey from the mouth of the Vitim across the Lena gold fields to Chita. He discovered the Patom and Vitim Plateaus, for which he ultimately received the Russian Geographical Society's Gold Medal.[98] The 1866 Olekminsk-Vitimsk expedition capped a three-year effort to work out an orographic scheme first suggested by his findings during the Manchurian adventure in 1864. His measurements of the mountains convinced him that Siberia from the Urals to the Pacific was not an extensive plain, as depicted on the maps, but rather a huge plateau cut through with mountain ranges. His conclusions were embodied in "A Report About Olekminsk-Vitimsk Expedition," presented to the Russian Geographicaal Society and published a few years later. The heights between the sources of the rivers Olekma and Nercha were ultimately named after Kropotkin. The road opened by Kropotkin in 1866 led to the economic development of the Lena gold fields.[99]

In January 1866 some Polish exiles in Siberia rose in an

unsuccessful insurrection. Peter followed their subsequent trial and sent accounts to St. Petersburg newspapers, for which he had been reporting on Siberian affairs since 1862, and exposed the brutalities inflicted on the Poles. Kropotkin interceded on their behalf to have their death sentences suspended and got the governor-general to promise not to execute them until a reprieve had been passed upon in St. Petersburg. However, the promise was not kept.[100] In part as a reaction, both Peter and Alexander determined to leave the army as quickly as possible.[101] Alexander had secured a post in Siberia in 1865 and in 1867 they both returned to St. Petersburg, thus ending the Siberian period for Peter, who would never return there.

In his *Memoirs* Peter spoke glowingly of the Siberian experience and credited it with being critical in his political development as a radical. Those years taught him the absolute impossibility of doing anything really useful for the mass of the people by means of an administrative machinery. They taught him to appreciate the constructive work of the unknown masses seldom mentioned in books:

> ... to live with natives, to see at work all the complex forms of social organization which they have elaborated far away from the influence of any civilization, was, as it were, to store up floods of light which illuminated my subsequent reading. The part which the unknown masses play in the accomplishment of all important historical events, and even in war, became evident to me from direct observation, and I came to hold ideas similar to those which Tolstoi expresses concerning the leaders and the masses in his monumental book *War and Peace*.[102]

As to the state of his political convictions as a result of five years in Siberia:

> Although I did not then formulate my observations in terms borrowed from party struggles, I may say now that I lost in Siberia whatever faith in state discipline I had cherished before. I was prepared to become an anarchist.[103]

III   *Kropotkin Becomes a Revolutionary*

Having left Siberia, the Kropotkin brothers settled in St. Petersburg. For the next three years Peter devoted himself to geography. He had a nominal position in the Ministry of the

Interior as of 1868. This status was retained until 1872. It got him out of the army and involved no duties. Alexander entered the military school of jurisprudence. Peter entered the university, studying mathematics and geography. He presented the report of his Vitim expedition to the Imperial Russian Geographical Society. Offered the Secretaryship of the Physical Geography section of the Geographical Society, a part-time position, he accepted gladly. He supplemented this small income by translating certain of Herbert Spencer's works.[104]

Peter's journeys in Siberia had convinced him that the mountains of Northern Siberia were wrongly depicted on the maps. The East Siberian ridges did not in fact exist; rather there were vast plateaus. The main structural lines of Asia, he believed, were not north and south, or west and east, but rather went from southwest to northeast. He hypothesized that the mountains of Asia were not bundles of independent ridges like the Alps but were subordinated to an immense plateau—indeed that they constituted an old continent which once pointed toward the Bering Straits. This theory he considered his chief contribution to science.[105]

In 1870 Peter was involved in a polar expedition project. He and three others worked out a plan. In the report Kropotkin ventured the opinion that to the north of Novaia Zemlia Island there should be undiscovered land which would stretch northward beyond Spitzbergen and which held back floating ice. This turned out to be correct: in 1873 an Austrian polar expedition discovered an entire archipelago there and named it Franz Josef Land.[106]

Peter's political interests at the time were stimulated by the Franco-Prussian War and the rise and fall of the Paris Commune. In 1871 he followed accounts of the famous Nechaev trial, and his notes show some familiarity with the then-leading anarchist, Michael Bakunin. Both he and Alexander went to meetings to discuss the Franco-Prussian War and the problem of the coming revolution.[107]

In the spring of 1871 he was commissioned to conduct a geographical investigation of Finland and Sweden. The goal of these investigations was to clarify the question of the Ice Age and to gather facts concerning his hypothesis about the Ice Age. Much would come of this trip's findings in his theory on the glaciation of Europe and its sculpting of the lakes of northeastern

basic ideas were: 1) the unavoidability of social revolution and 2) the necessity of a stateless organization of society. In the fall of 1872 Peter was told by the circle to work out a revolutionary program. At the time he favored focusing propaganda on the workers and peasants rather than on the students. Lebedev says that he was one of the first Russian revolutionaries to turn his attention to urban workers, especially in St. Petersburg and among the weavers of Narva Gate.[123]

Peter participated in the circle some two years before his arrest. Sophia Perovskaia hosted many of its meetings.[124] Dmitri Klements was Peter's closest friend at the university, and it was he who introduced Peter to the circle.[125] Klements, Kravchinsky, and Kropotkin were considered to be the group's best propagandists but according to Kravchinsky, Peter was incapable of commanding or organizing anyone, although both Kravchinsky and I. M. Maisky corroborate that Peter was already a fiery and spellbinding speaker.[126]

At one point early in his association with the circle, he was asked to contribute some of his personal wealth to subsidize it. He refused, alleging it would be better to save it for a more important time, say when the workers took to arms. While one might be somewhat wary of crediting this excuse, it is clear that he saw the moderate majority of the circle, mostly Lavrovites, as gearing their approach to students, which he felt was wrong. For Kropotkin felt by this time that the useful life was not lived by academics or professionals. This meant opting for Bakunin over Lavrov.[127]

The young intelligentsia were suspect in his eyes as reluctant to give up their privileges. Hence the revolutionary appeal must be directed primarily to the masses. Kropotkin's thinking now showed a populist strain. He grudgingly allowed the intelligentsia a propagandist role but only because there were few agitators as yet from the ranks of the people. He laid stress on federated agrarian communes and looked upon Western political institutions as formalistic. He believed in a Russian revolutionary party.[128] Certainly he represented the revolutionary left of the circle. He was, according to Tikhomirov, interested in immediate uprisings, not just propagandizing.[129]

Peter completed his first major political study, "Should we occupy ourselves with examining the Ideal Future Order?" in November 1873. It was meant to be a memorandum for discussion within the circle. It contained in skeletal form many of the ideas he would later elaborate into more comprehensive approaches to social reconstruction. It starts from the premise that all means of production and capital will become common property and that the labor process must be reorganized along egalitarian lines: all direct producers must run their factories and there must be no privileged categories of workers. Manual labor will be the duty of all men. Education will be universal and combine intellectual and vocational aspects. Labor must be useful, that is, it must answer a need of society. It must be useful to the majority.[130] He rejects the state and suggests the use of labor checks instead of money. As to his revolutionary strategy, Kropotkin explicitly rejects Nechaev's conspiratorial ideas. Revolutionaries cannot make revolutions, but they can channel the scattered efforts of the dissatisfied and they can reinforce this dissatisfaction through propaganda. Interestingly, he saw little point at the time in joining the International because the movement was still too weak.[131] He emphasized again and again that revolutionaries must be willing to live at the level of the common man and that agitators from the people were more effective than those from the civilized milieu.[132]

At the end of 1873 Perovskaia and other members of the circle were arrested.[133] Meanwhile Peter had been living a double life, agitating and simultaneously working on his geographical treatises. On March 23, 1874, he was arrested by the Third Section, the Tsarist secret police. Just that month, he had delivered a final report to the Geographical Society on his theory of the Ice Age. The society, recognizing the importance of the theory, had elected him president of its Physical and Mathematical Department. The following day, on the personal order of Alexander II, he was placed in the Peter and Paul fortress. The arrest scandalized the capital. The horror of a former *page de chambre*'s having become a revolutionary accounted for a visit to his cell by the Tsar's brother, the Grand Prince Nikolai, who tried to discover what he believed. Peter refused to enlighten him.[134] The Tsar acceded to the pleas of friends and the Geographical Society to allow him books and writing materials so he could complete his report on the glaciation of Europe. Peter was to remain a prisoner for two years.[135] In mid-June Alexander arrived from Geneva after learning of Peter's arrest. He wrote to Lavrov in December

1874, three days after writing Peter in celebration of his thirty-second birthday. The letter to Lavrov was intercepted by the police and used as a basis for Alexander's arrest on December 29, 1874. On May 13, 1875, Alexander was sentenced to administrative exile in northeast Siberia. He left Petersburg on May 22, 1875. Alexander committed suicide there in 1886.[136]

Of his brother Peter wrote in his *Memoirs* that he had not taken part in the agitation, did not believe in the possibility of a popular uprising, and conceived of a revolution only as the action of a representative body. The brothers would not meet again after Alexander's arrest. Sister Helen visited Peter in prison at the end of December 1874. She and her sister-in-law were arrested after Peter's escape but were soon released.[137]

In March 1876 Peter was transferred to the House of Detention, a new prison in St. Petersburg, because of ill health—he had contracted scurvy at one point. In large measure his transfer to the military hospital was due to Helen's great efforts.[138] From this minimal-security prison, with the aid of friends, he escaped on June 30, 1876. The whole episode of the escape, its planning and execution, is revealed in some detail by Kropotkin in his *Memoirs*. He escaped via Finland and Sweden and then to Norway, and from there to England (Edinburgh) in August 1876.[139] He used the pseudonym Alexis Levashov.[140] While he could read and write English, he could not speak it or understand spoken English.[141]

IV   *Kropotkin's Career in Western Europe*

In September he moved to London, where he approached the junior editor, James Scott Keltie, of the journal *Nature*, in order to find work writing scientific notes.[142] Having long corresponded with James Guillaume, he was cordially received on his arrival in Neuchatel, Switzerland, in December 1876. There he met the Italian anarchists Carlo Cafiero and Errico Malatesta. He traveled to Belgium and then back to Zurich, where he met his old friend Dmitri Klements.[143] It was at this time that he first met the French communard émigré and eminent geographer Elisee Reclus, destined to become one of his closest friends.

Kropotkin decided to identify with the Jura Federation, whose leading light was Guillaume. It was then the ideological center of European anarchism. After Paul Brousse's anarchist paper

(published in Berne and to which Kropotkin had made contributions) had been suppressed in 1876, Kropotkin undertook the
editing of the Jura Federation organ.

In 1878 Kropotkin met his future wife in a Geneva cafeteria
frequented by Russian students.[144] She was twenty-two, came
from a Russian Jewish family, and was studying biology in Berne.
They were married on October 8, 1878. It was to be a very happy
marriage despite the significant age difference,[145] although Sofia
would play no role in Peter's intellectual life. There would be
one child, Alexandra, born in England in April 1887.

In February 1879 he began a fortnightly in Geneva, *Le
Revolté*, most of which he had to write himself.[146] In *Le Revolté*
of November 1879 Kropotkin published an article which marked
the beginnings of his anarchist-communism. Essentially
anarchist-communism means that distribution is on the basis of
need rather than according to work, as the Bakuninists'
collectivism indicated. The term was first used by the French
communard exile in Geneva Francois Dumartheray in 1876
without any exposition on his part and thereafter utilized by
Italian anarchist organizations. Kropotkin remained ignorant of it
until 1879. Not until 1880 was it written into the Programme of
Jura Federation as a result of Kropotkin's persistence. Kropotkin,
while not having had anything to do with the origination of the
theory became its greatest exponent.[147] His most famous
pamphlet, "An Appeal to the Young," first appeared in *Le
Revolté* in 1880. It was reprinted as a brochure in 1881.[148]

After the assassination of Alexander II on March 1, 1881, the
Russian government, considering Kropotkin one of the instiga-
tors, demanded his expulsion from Switzerland. In July 1881 the
Swiss complied, forbidding Kropotkin to return.[149] The Holy
League, a reactionary Tsarist organization, passed a sentence of
death on him for his alleged part in the assassination.[150] He now
relocated to France in the small town of Tonon near Lake
Geneva, so that his wife could complete her studies in
Switzerland. He collaborated with Elisee Reclus at this time. In
the summer of 1881 Kropotkin learned that the Holy League
intended to assassinate him. At this point Kropotkin moved to
London. There he spent almost a year but was unhappy, and in
the fall of 1882 he returned to Tonon. The French, who were
attempting to form an alliance with Russia against Germany,
decided to appease the Russian government by arresting

Kropotkin. The French papers played up Kropotkin as a dangerous agitator just come from England to manage the workers' movement. In December 1882 he was arrested along with some comrades from Lyons. In January 1883 a Lyons court gave him a five-year sentence for belonging to the International, which had been outlawed under a law dating from the suppression of the Paris Commune. In fact, the International no longer existed.[151]

In March 1883 Kropotkin was sent from the Lyons prison to the central penitentiary in Clairvaux. A group of deputies in the French Parliament agitated for his immediate release and a group of outstanding scientists and public figures including Herbert Spencer, the poet Victor Hugo, and Ernest Renan petitioned the French government to annul the sentence. At Clairvaux he was allowed to continue his scientific work although nothing was published during his sentence. The French Academy of Science made their library available to him, Sofia kept him supplied with books, and Ernest Renan made his personal library available as well. Despite the relative comforts of Clairvaux, his health deteriorated. He suffered from malaria and scurvy. The French press now took up the case for his release, but only when his health deteriorated further, in January 1886, did the French government decide to free him. That spring of 1886 he left France for England, where he resided until 1917, leaving only for short trips to Switzerland, Italy, and, after 1905, to France.[152] He also made two short trips to North America.

While Kropotkin was in Clairvaux, Elisee Reclus published a compilation of his articles that had appeared in *Le Revolté* from 1879-1882. The anthology was called *Paroles d'un Révolté*.[153] It presented his views on the tactics and strategy of the coming revolution, on the agrarian question, on the role of the masses, and some thoughts on the future society. It constitutes one of the very best sources of his analysis of the revolutionary process.

During his Clairvaux imprisonment Kropotkin began to realize the demoralizing effect of prisons on prisoners. He wrote in his *Memoris*:

Whole generations of future criminals are bred in these nurseries, which the state supports and which society tolerates, simply because it does not want to hear its own diseases spoken of and dissected ... imprisonment is in an immense number of cases a punishment which bears far more severely upon quite innocent people, than upon the condemned prisoner himself.[154]

The prison regime destroys a man's will and his energy. It creates a dislike of work:

What a nest of infecton is every prison—and every law court—for its neighborhood, for the people who live near it. Lombroso has made much of the "criminal type" which he believes he has discovered amongst the inmates of the prisons. If he had made the same efforts to observe the people who hang about the law courts—detectives, spies, petty solicitors, informers, people preying upon the simpletons, and the like, he would probably have concluded that his criminal type has a far greater geographical extension than the prison walls.[155]

Kropotkin would write in 1887 a book on the themes of the impossibility of humane prisons and the futility of prison reforms entitled *In Russian and French Prisons.*

After his release, the Kropotkins settled in the London suburb of Harrow, finding two old friends, Kravchinsky and Chaivkovsky, in England. They were also reunited with Alexander's widow and son who came to live with Kropotkin in London.[156] In October 1886 the first issue of *Freedom* appeared. It was the first English anarchist paper and Kropotkin helped found it.[157] He would be associated with it for the next twenty-eight years.[158]

In England Kropotkin's "circle" included William Morris, W. B. Yeats, Oscar Wilde, William Rossetti, Ford Maddox Ford, and G. B. Shaw in addition to the Russians. The head of the Independent Labor party, Keir Hardie, remained a close friend of Kropotkin despite his resistance to Peter's preaching against the parliamentary illusion. From 1893 to 1905 Kropotkin wrote articles regularly for the *Geographical Journal.* His friend Keltie continued to provide him with income for his articles published in *Nature.* Keltie, in addition to being assistant editor of *Nature,* was secretary of the Royal Geographical Society. Patrick Geddes, James Mavor, and Robertson Smith were academic friends, the latter a professor at Cambridge and editor of the *Encyclopaedia Britannica.* There is a famous story that, through Smith, Kropotkin was offered a professorship of Geography at Cambridge on condition that he renounce his anarchist allegiance, which he refused to do. According to Mavor this is not so. There was no offer because they assumed he would refuse to compromise his freedom of action by taking it.[159]

Kropotkin wrote a series of articles on the organization of social life according to the principles of anarchist-communism. The articles were published in the Paris anarchist journal *La Revolté*, the successor to *Le Revolté*, and in 1892 these articles and essays were reworked by Kropotkin and put together in a book entitled *La Conquéte du Pain*.[160] His research and thoughts on industrial organization, the trend toward centralization of industry during the industrializing period, and what he believed to be the countertrend toward self-sufficiency among former colonial and industrially dependent countries first gave rise to a series of articles published in the *Nineteenth Century* from 1888 to 1890. The articles discussed possibilities of decentralization of production, economic regionalism, integration of industry and agriculture and of mental and physical work as well as the fullest exploration of science to lessen manual labor and maximize productivity in all spheres. Much of this found its way into the book *Fields, Factories and Workshops*, published in 1899.[161]

Simultaneously with his economic research in the period 1889–1898, Kropotkin began research on the role and significance in social and animal life of mutual aid. He had become interested in the idea in Siberia after having read Darwin's *Origin of Species*. Observing the wild creatures in Siberia, he had sought to confirm the Darwinist law of struggle for existence. He observed among species like wild deer and birds mutual support as well as struggle. A speech by the Russian zoologist Professor Kessler, given at a Congress of Natural Scientists in 1880, re-animated these speculations. According to Kessler, mutual aid is a natural law as is mutual struggle, but for the progressive development of the species the first law is incomparably more important than the second. Kropotkin was intellectually aroused to the point of embarking on a serious study in 1888 by what he considered an abuse of Darwinian theory:

When Huxley published in 1888 his atrocious article, "The Struggle for Existence; a Program," I decided to put in a readable form my objections to his way of understanding the struggle for life, among animals as well as among men, the materials for which I had been accumulating for two years. I spoke of it to my friends. However, I found that the interpretation of "struggle for life" in the sense of a war cry or "woe to the weak," raised to the height of a commandment of nature revealed by science, was so deeply rooted in the country that it had become almost a matter of religion.[162]

The editor of the *Nineteenth Century*, James Knowles, and H. W. Bates, the secretary of the Geographical Society, supported Kropotkin in his desire to refute this interpretation. The result was a series of articles in the *Nineteenth Century*.[163] According to Woodcock and Avakumovic, Knowles was the first man, apart from Bates and Geddes and outside socialist circles, to see immediately the point of Kropotkin's evolutionary ideas and to encourage the project.[164] The articles spanned the period 1890-1896. In 1902 all of them were collected and published in a book entitled *Mutual Aid—A Factor of Evolution*. Two years later the Russian language edition appeared to be followed by translations into all the major European languages.[165]

Along with the *Conquest of Bread* and *Fields, Factories and Workshops*, *Mutual Aid* represents the most significant and influential of Kropotkin's books. His thesis, supported by voluminous documentation from biological observations, is that in the animal world the tendency or instinct for cooperation within a given species is more decisive than the struggle for existence, that mutual aid and solidarity among both animals and men is the main factor in social and animal life and that it alone insures social progress and the promotion of higher culture. In recognizing mutual aid as the main factor in human evolution and progress, Kropotkin does not deny the importance of struggle. He emphasizes that popularizers and unscrupulous ideologues anxious to invoke Darwin and natural science to justify a competitive and aggressive social order had either consciously or unconsciously distorted *Origin of Species*. Kropotkin sees himself as rescuing Darwinism from social Darwinism. *Mutual Aid* is to prove central to his subsequent political theorizing, which substantially bases itself on a view of human nature keyed to its thesis.

During 1889, Kropotkin focused his research primarily on the French Revolution. He wrote a series of articles for *Le Revolté* and a long essay, "The Great French Revolution and Its Lessons," for the *Nineteenth Century*. These proved to be preliminary sketches for a major work entitled *The Great Revolution*, which was published in both English and French in 1909.

From about 1890, while continuing as a regular contributor to *Freedom*, Kropotkin no longer performed editorial duties. Woodcock and Avakumovic felt that after 1890, especially after 1894, he had ceased to be an agitator and pamphleteer and had become a scholarly recluse. As the 1890s progressed, his characteristic tone of extreme revolutionary optimism faded though revived briefly by the 1905 revolution in Russia. During these years he was more concerned with social construction and scientific and ethical problems than with revolutionary actions.[166]

In 1893 the British Scientific Association in honor of his services selected Kropotkin for membership, and that year he delivered his report on the Ice Age to their congress. Since the congress was to be held in Toronto, Canada, in 1897, Kropotkin made his first trip to North America. After the congress, in the company of the famous German geologist Renk and the Canadian professor Snaiders, he traveled throughout Canada. The trip had some practical effects. When in 1898 Russian Dukhobors, members of a dissident religious sect originating in the eighteenth century, decided to emigrate, Kropotkin published an article in the *Nineteenth Century* expressing the view that northwest Canada because of its climate and soil would be a suitable place for them. Tolstoi wrote to Kropotkin, asking him to facilitate the resettlement of the Dukhobors. Kropotkin turned to his old friend James Mavor, a professor of geography at the University of Toronto, who was influential in finalizing arrangements with the Canadian government. And in 1899, 7,500 Dukhobors duly emigrated.[167]

The trip included a visit to Mennonite agricultural communities in Western Canada. Kropotkin blithely attributed their excellent economic performance to their communistic tendencies, despite their practices lacking any communal cultivation or distribution.

Kropotkin crossed over into the United States, touring Chicago, Philadelphia, New York, Boston, and Washington. He traveled to Pittsburgh, hoping to see Alexander Berkman, the anarchist imprisoned for shooting Frick, but he was in solitary confinement. He met the "mad bomber," Johan Most, in New York as well as the leader of the American anarchist individualist school, Benjamin Tucker. In Boston, Walter Hines Page persuaded the reluctant publishers of the *Atlantic Monthly* to commission Kropotkin's memoirs as a series of monthly essays.[168] They first appeared in book form as *Memoirs of a Revolutionist* in 1898 and have since become a classic source on Russian and European revolutionary and social currents of the nineteenth century. Kropotkin ends his *Memoirs* at age fifty-seven.

In March 1901 he made a second trip to America. This time he was invited by the Lowell Institute in Boston to give a series of lectures on Russian literature. These lectures were, in 1905, published under the title *Ideals and Realities in Russian Literature*. The book is not without interest to the student of Russian literature although, as might have been expected, it is imbued with the social and political views of its author and hence the perspective is slanted more toward social and political values than aesthetic ones. Of the great Russian novelists, Kropotkin is kindest to Turgenev, whom he knew in Paris, and Tolstoi, with whom he corresponded. He is extremely ill-disposed toward Dostoevsky and especially *The Brothers Karamazov*, probably because he disliked Dostoevsky's political views. In any event, his evaluations in this case have not stood the test of time. Of *The Brothers Karamazov*, considered one of the greatest novels ever written, and of Dostoevsky in general he wrote:

Whatsoever a certain portion of contemporary critics, fond of all sorts of morbid literature, may have written about this novel, the present writer can only say that he found it, all through, so unnatural, so much fabricated—here, a bit of morals, there some abominable character taken from a psychopathological hospital or again, in order to analyze the feelings of some purely imaginary criminal, that a few good pages scattered here and there do not compensate the reader for the hard task of reading. . . .
The artistic qualities of his novels are incomparably below those of any one of the great Russian masters: Tolstoi, Turgueneff, or Gontcharoff.
. . . Every one of the heroes of Dostoyevsky, especially in his novels of the later period, is a person suffering from some psychological disease or from moral perversion.[169]

In November 1901 Kropotkin suffered a heart attack. By 1903, he had sufficiently recovered and was involved in constructing a theory of the foundation of the Asian continent and another on the ice age. But he was forced into bed in late 1904.[170] Still, he did keep up in these years with the anarchist movement. In July

1902 he wrote Guillaume that the syndicalist movement in France was creating optimism and that perhaps a new International might be created. In 1905 he met Guillaume in Brittany. His friend had become a syndicalist and was enthusiastic about the recent foundation of the Confederacion General du Travail (CGT). Kropotkin did not regard the unions as capable of creating an anarchist society. Local and communal organizations would have to provide the bridges between industries.[171]

In 1904 Kropotkin wrote an essay on "The Ethical Needs of the Present Day." With his earlier pamphlet on "Anarchist Morality,"[172] this turned out to be a sketch for his *Ethics*, published posthumously, which he began work on in Dmitrov in 1918-19. In *Ethics*, Kropotkin tried to answer two fundamental moral questions: From where do man's moral conceptions originate? What are the purposes of moral standards? Kropotkin regarded ethics as the physics of human conduct and as a concrete, scientific discipline whose object was to improve men in their practical activities. He denied any religious or metaphysical basis for morality and, in the planned study, was attempting to establish ethics on a purely naturalistic basis.[173]

In the 1890s Kropotkin had increasingly feared German militarism. He saw Bismarckian-Prussian state worship as the ultimate in reactionary European politics. Thus in 1905 he urged the French anarchists to drop their anticonscription and antimilitarism line.[174] It seems that Kropotkin's later pro-French attitude on the outbreak of World War I could be traced to this period. Certainly he expressed an inordinate love of France as the cradle of the modern revolutionary tradition, a love testified to by his work on the Great French Revolution and the emotional impact on him of the Paris Commune. In 1907 Kropotkin's failure to come to the International Anarchist Convention in Amsterdam may have been due to his increasing tendency toward what Woodcock and Avakumovic call "a kind of mitigated French patriotism." The Convention strongly condemned any service in the army.[175]

Kropotkin's relation to the Russian revolutionary movement after escaping from Russia was minimal at best. He was certainly an actor in the West European revolutionary movement but this did not insure any influence in Russia. In the early 1890s his pamphlets first appeared in Russian in Switzerland. In 1902 in Geneva there appeared the first Russian anarchist paper, *Khleb i*

Volia, and he contributed to it.[176] But there was the issue of terrorism dividing him from the Russian revolutionaries, both populist and anarchist. Kropotkin had objected to their changing the emphasis in the late 1870s from popular agitation to political assassination and terrorism.[177] Kropotkin personally abhorred violence although he realized that it was justified against a violent system. He refused to condemn anarchist assassins, although he felt their "deeds"—so-called propaganda of the deed—were at times counterproductive and in general inefficacious. In this light Turgenev's denial to Kropotkin's niece that Kropotkin had anything to do with serving as a model or inspiration for Bazarov in *Fathers and Sons* seems unnecessary. Turgenev added that Kropotkin was incapable of a terrorist act and Kropotkin's attitude on terror was made clear in his opposition to the terrorist *Narodnaia Volia*, the leftwing of the Russian Social Revolutionary underground. He felt that the main struggle must be economic. He was not against terror, but it had to be merely supplementary to agitation among the people.[178]

According to his most recent biographer, he ultimately resolved his ambivalence on the question of political terrorism by distinguishing deliberate individual terrorism from spontaneous mass violence, condemning those who interpreted the anarchist tactic of "propaganda by the deed" as a license to murder statesmen indiscriminately.[179]

With the opening of the Russo-Japanese War in 1904, social unrest in Russia escalated. Kropotkin was approached by Japanese agents in 1904 with the bait of money if he would serve their cause. He refused.[180] This was not due to some residual sense of Russian patriotism. Rather it was a matter of revolutionary principle. He believed that the means employed must be consonant with the end. On the same basis he opposed in principle the tactic of expropriation, that is, armed robberies of banks, etc., for the sake of subsidizing the anarchist cause. This was his position at the London anarchist conference in 1904. His reasoning was that expropriation violated the work principle: only labor would be a source of income. In fact, there was no resolution adopted on expropriation at the conference since, consistent with anarchist principles, all decisions had to be unanimous.[181]

The Russian revolution of 1905 excited Kropotkin and gave him hopes of a return to Russia. He considered it a first victory with more to follow. It was seen as combining the two main elements, peasants and workers, in one revolutionary wave. The most remarkable aspect of the revolution, he wrote in a pamphlet of that year, was the conspicuous absence of professional revolutionaries from the spontaneous event. He felt it was difficult to predict how far the social revolution would go. For the first time Kropotkin's views were officially allowed publication in Russia. Maxim Gorky in 1906 began to edit Kropotkin's works in Russian but the project was aborted by the Tsarist government as it regained its confidence.[182]

In October 1905 Kropotkin wrote a letter to the anarchist Goldsmit expressing the hope that the newspaper *Khleb i Volia* would become the organ for a serious anarchist party in Russia. Kropotkin had a great desire to return to Russia in late 1905 and again in early 1906 but the reaction foiled any possibility. The Georgian émigré anarchist Gogelia had published *Khleb i Volia*, but he returned to Russia in 1905 and publication ceased. Kropotkin then organized a successor in Paris called *Listi Khlebi i Voli*, a weekly.[183] He was to remain active on the editorial board.

Kropotkin had to take a stand on a most important tactical question during the 1905 revolution: Should the anarchists join the councils or soviets that had sprung up in the major Russian cities? Would they, in doing so, lend themselves to a statist institution? His answer was a qualified assent: yes, if the soviets were organs of struggle against the bourgeoisie and the state and not organs of rule. As for himself, he would personally prefer to remain within the working masses.[184] In the glow of the revolution of 1905, Kropotkin in 1906 advocated that all land should go to the communes, which would deal with its use and distribution. Factories, workshops, and transportation should be run not by new ministries as proposed by the Social Democrats, but by the workers organized in free unions or syndicates.[185] In October 1906 Kropotkin attended a small Russian anarchist congress in London, where he delivered two reports: one on "Our Relation to the Peasant and Workers' Union" and another on "The Political and Economic Revolution." In the first he expressed support for the anarchists joining the unions to help develop the workers' movement. Under his influence the congress passed a resolution against "partial expropriation," essentially saying that the main force of the revolution must be in the moral sphere.[186]

Kropotkin in 1906 became ill again and in 1909 moved from Bromley to the small town of Brighton for health reasons. Here he convalesced and began work on *The Great French Revolution*, which he finished in the spring of 1909. It was a pioneering effort to describe the revolution from the standpoint of the masses, focusing on the peasant uprising and city insurrections. Kropotkin was the first historian of the revolution to emphasize the tremendous role of the Paris sections. The book led to investigations of the special role of the Paris sections by Professor Oliara and the Russian professor N. I. Kareev,[187] who comments that Kropotkin turned more attention to ideology than to economics.[188] The germ of the idea of focusing on the role of the masses was contained in a review Kropotkin did of a book on the revolution by E. Taine in 1878. *The Great French Revolution* was a favorite of Lenin's, who urged that it be translated into Russian in a personal meeting with Kropotkin in May 1919. Kropotkin objected to the state's publishing it and Lenin countered by saying that the cooperative press could do it. Kropotkin agreed on condition that it be sold at a cheap price.[189]

In 1907 a Bolshevik congress met in London. Lenin, M. Litvinov, E. Yaroslavsky, V. Nogin, K. Voroshilov, and Stalin were present. Kropotkin was among the attending guests. The Bolsheviks were invited to tea at the Kropotkins' and a lively polemic ensued.[190]

In July of 1907, due to a recurrence of ill health, Kropotkin abandoned the editorship of *Listi Khlebi i Voli*. It expired in 1910. Its successor was *Rabochi Mir*, established in 1911. It became the organ of the Federation of Russian Anarchist Communists in 1913 but suspended publication at the beginning of the First World War. Kropotkin's regular contributions represented a revival of political effort since he had mentioned in a letter to his friend Goldsmit in 1908 that he was too old to keep active journalistically and that he wanted to work on his theoretical works on socialism and anarchism.[191] Later he would help put together Bakunin's collected works for publication.[192]

Kropotkin in 1909 wrote a "fact book" exposing and documenting Tsarist political oppression. It was entitled *The Terror in Russia* and sponsored by the British Parliamentary Russian Committee. The main focus was on the conditions in Russian prisons and among the political exiles. The expository style is free of any anarchist or even socialist tone. In the introduction he writes:

The present conditions in Russia are so desperate that it is a public duty to lay before this country a statement of these conditions, with a solemn appeal to all lovers of liberty and progress for moral support in the struggle that is now going on for the conquest of political freedom.

In the struggle for freedom each country must work out its own solution; but we should not forget that there exists a web of international solidarity between all civilized countries.[193]

Kropotkin took as his point of departure the October 1905 Tsarist declaration granting civil liberties and representative government. He noted that those who took this seriously and acted on it were being prosecuted. The result was large numbers of prosecutions, overcrowded prisons with alarming types of epidemics and unspeakable sanitary conditions. Mass starvation and unemployment seemed to be part of deliberate policy, along with official brutality toward prisoners.[194] The ill-treatment of those condemned to death has led to epidemics of suicide.[195] Wholesale and illegal flogging of peasants in order to collect arrears is practiced on a grand scale.[196] In conclusion he writes:

Suffering and martyrdom are certainly unavoidable in every struggle for freedom. But the amount of suffering and cruel repression now prevalent in Russia surpasses everything that is known from the lessons of modern history. . . . Despotism in one part of the world reacts upon all the races of the world. And when it takes such brutal and mediaeval forms as it takes in Russian prisons and in the punitive expeditions, by means of which autocracy is maintained in the Russian Empire, all mankind feels the effect of such a return to the horrors of the Dark Ages.[197]

Kropotkin's seventieth birthday fell on December 9, 1912. Celebrations were planned in Paris and London. In the London jubilee meeting Bernard Shaw spoke in honor of Kropotkin.[198]

In 1913 Kropotkin published *Contemporary Science and Anarchism.* In it he likened society to an individual organism which is a federation of different organs. Nowhere in the organic world is there a directing center to which all parts subordinate themselves. In political life he pointed out that the main factor in history was the creative role of the masses. The book also delved into the origins of the state and its role in history.[199]

When World War I broke out, Kropotkin split the anarchist movement by taking a defensive position in favor of France. In

Russia, however, the Russian anarchists followed a defeatist line, as did a majority of the anarchist Russian émigrés. Lenin, in 1914, lashed out at Kropotkin as well as the Marxist George Plekhanov, calling them chauvinists.[200] Lenin wrote an article in Geneva in 1916 entitled "On Problems of Opportunism in France," in which he condemned anarchist patriots and chauvinists like Kropotkin.[201] Malatesta had written a letter to *Freedom* deploring Kropotkin's position as a negation of anarchism.[202] Two biographers quite friendly to Kropotkin, Planche and Delphy, felt that Malatesta's case against Kropotkin had an implacable logic.[203] Kropotkin was not alone. Jean Grave, Charles Malato, Paul Reclus (Elisee's son), and Christian Cornelissen supported him. In 1916, Grave and Kropotkin wrote a prowar manifesto, "The Manifesto of the 16," which was signed *inter alia* by Guerin, Cherkesov, Malato, Cornelissen, and Paul Reclus. Those opposing the war included Malatesta, Shapiro, Domela Niewenhuis, Emma Goldman, Berkman, Bertoni, Yanovsky, and Rocker.[204] According to M. Perro, Kropotkin's reluctance to polemicize over the issue was because he considered his position so irresistible.[205] G. Sandomirsky ascribes his "ententophilism," in part, to a need to save his belief in France's revolutionary role. He points out that Kropotkin remained an apologist for Versailles and France even after 1917. He was a vigorous proponent of the return to Alsace-Lorraine to France.[206]

V   *Last Years in Russia*

From the first days of the Russian revolution, Kropotkin determined to return to Russia. After the February revolution, he urged the new government to continue the war. Woodcock and Avakumovic feel that his anti-Germanism blinded him. He wrote an appeal in April 1917 for the "Liberty Loan" and in May accepted the chairmanship of the Correct Information Committee, whose purpose it was to provide facts and information reflecting favorably on the new Russian regime. Kropotkin felt that the revolution was based on patriotism and that the wartime organizations represented a step towards free communism.[207]

On June 12, 1917, Kropotkin arrived in Petrograd via Bergen, Norway, Sweden and Finland. The provisional government offered him a post and a yearly pension, both of which he refused on anarchist principles. Kropotkin had four meetings with Prince

Lvov, in which the offer of a portfolio in the Kerensky government came up again.[208] He intended to live in Petrograd, but he fell ill and his doctor advised him to go to Moscow. He arrived there in July. He found a two-room apartment only to lose it after the October revolution, when it was requisitioned.[209] His daughter and her husband, N. V. Lebedev, had already moved to Russia a few years earlier and had met him in Petrograd.[210]

In Moscow in 1917 he expressed the belief that the revolution would run its logical course, realizing the ideals of communism and federalism. And it was in this spirit that he welcomed the October revolution. He wrote to a friend in December 1918 that the communists were true socialists and in another letter of January 1919 that the Social Democrats felt that the people were not ready for a social revolution but that the Bolsheviks thought otherwise and they were right.[211] Kropotkin however had been lending his prestige to the more moderate cause in 1917. According to David Shub, the Bolsheviks' unsuccessful July putsch upset him deeply, as did the resignation of Prince Lvov, the provisional government's first premier and a liberal. At the national State Conference in Moscow in August 1917, Kropotkin looked forward to the November elections to the Constituent Assembly.[212] Kropotkin's speech at the State Conference equated the defense of Russia with the defense of the revolution and called for the declaration of a Russian Republic modeled on the U.S. system of local autonomy.[213] He had attended the Constituent Assembly, calling on the capitalists to join in building the new society. He was in favor of proclaiming a republic. He was working with the League of Federalists in producing federalist literature in 1918.[214] In Moscow, in 1918, he was visited by anarchists G. P. Maximov, Alexander Shapiro, and Voline. In the summer of 1918, the day before moving from Moscow to Dmitrov, he received a chance visit from Nester Makhno, the anarchist guerrilla leader in the Ukraine.[215] Voline reports that Makhno greatly appreciated certain of Kropotkin's suggestions.[216]

In the summer of 1918 Kropotkin and family were compelled to leave Moscow for Dmitrov. He often remarked that he felt totally cut off from the world there. He began work on *Ethics* but needed access to books. His entire library had been left in London. He could not afford a secretary. The poor rations available undermined his delicate health. The house was not electrified and he had to work at night by kerosene lamp, and there was a kerosene shortage. Only in 1920 would the house be electrified.[217]

His relations with the Bolsheviks were not good. He was treated with deference but kept isolated in Dmitrov. He turned down royalties from his books which had been published.[218] He had turned down the provisional government's offer to head the Ministry of Education and he refused in any way to associate himself with the Bolshevik government of 1918. From the Bolshevik perspective, he was obstructionist. He never recognized the necessity for the dictatorship of the proletariat. He underestimated the armed threat to the revolution. He had been naive in wanting the capitalists to help build a new society. From 1918 on he had written Lenin numerous letters expressing his opposition to the use of the Cheka's (secret police) terror. He had criticized the soviets for losing their autonomy. He called for mass development of cooperatives of all kinds independent of the state. Lenin or one of his representatives supposedly responded to each of his letters.[219]

In 1919 Emma Goldman visited the Kropotkins in Dmitrov. Peter, Sofia, and Alexandra were all living in one poorly heated room. Peter had refused a 250,000 ruble offer from the Soviet government for the right to issue his literary work. Behind his back, Sofia had accepted the Soviet Minister of Education's offer of an academic ration, knowing he would reject it. Alexander Berkman had accompanied Emma and Kropotkin told Berkman that he had not fully realized to what proportions the Marxian menace would grow. The Bolsheviks had become poisoned not so much by Marxism as by the Jesuitical spirit of its dogmas. The Bolshevik dictatorship had now, in his view, surpassed the autocracy of the Inquisition. The problem was, said Kropotkin, that one could not protest effectively at this stage because it would only give comfort to the external enemies of the revolution, the reactionary interventionists.[220] In July 1921 Goldman had again visited the Kropotkins and Peter had ventured the judgment that the Russian revolution was far greater than the French but that the Bolsheviks were the Jesuits of socialism.[221]

In May 1919 Kropotkin and Lenin met in Moscow in what proved to be their one and only meeting. David Shub believes that Kropotkin was attempting to save an old friend and colleague taken as a hostage and scheduled to be shot. According to the Bolshevik functionary V. D. Bonch-Bruevich, who arranged the meeting, Lenin had closely followed Kropotkin's living conditions. Kropotkin had requested the meeting, which took place at Bonch-Bruevich's apartment. Kropotkin told Lenin that while he, Kropotkin, esteemed cooperatives, Lenin obviously did not. Lenin denied this. Kropotkin claimed that bureaucracy was stifling the local cooperative in Dmitrov. When Kropotkin went on about the cooperative movement in England and syndicalism in France, Lenin denigrated these developments as wholly unable to change the social systems there. After Kropotkin left, Lenin remarked on how fresh and young Kropotkin's books were.[222] According to Shub, Kropotkin not only pleaded for his comrade, but asked Lenin to abolish the entire system of taking hostages and shooting people in reprisal for oppositionalist activity. Kropotkin later told his friend Dr. Alexander Atabekian that his comparison of the Red Terror to the Committee of Public Safety in the French Revolution which had killed so many outstanding revolutionaries had scared Lenin a little.[223]

In 1919, Kropotkin received a visit from Pestaña the representative of the Spanish Federation of labor. Pestaña asked Lenin why Alexandra Kropotkin was not allowed to leave the country. Lenin was embarrassed and gave Pestaña a written approval for her exit. However, the Cheka refused to honor it.[224]

Kropotkin wrote a letter to Lenin dated March 4, 1920, reciting details of the breakdown of supplies to the localities and the misery this was causing in the provinces. This he attributed to the centralized dictatorship:

> Even if a party dictatorship were the proper means to strike a blow at the capitalist system (which I thoroughly doubt), it is positively harmful for the building of a new socialist one. What is needed is local construction by local forces. Yet this is absent. ... Such construction below ... would be best undertaken by the Soviets. But Russia has already become a Soviet Republic only in name. ... At present, it is not the Soviets which rule in Russia but party committees and their constructive ability suffers from all the inefficiencies of bureaucratic organization.[225]

A second letter to Lenin, dated December 21, 1920, protested the taking of Socialist Revolutionary and White Guard hostages and the policy of executing them in case of attempts on the lives of Soviet leaders. It rebuked Lenin for the return to the worst practices of the Dark Ages and religious wars, terming such a policy unworthy of men who have undertaken to build a future commual society. He reminded Lenin that this was torture for the prisoners and their families. He chided Lenin: "Even Kings and Popes have rejected such barbarous means of defense as the taking of hostages." He ended with a plea not to tarnish the October Revolution which, with all its defects, has shown Western Europe that a social revolution is not impossible.[226]

In "A Message to the Workers of the West," dated June 10, 1920, and delivered to a visiting British Labor delegation, Kropotkin tells all Western workers to induce their governments to abandon the idea of armed intervention in the affairs of Russia. Every attempt at this merely results in a "reinforcement of the dictatorial tendencies of the rulers, and multiplies tenfold the natural evils of State Communism." He reiterates his condemnation of the Dictatorship of the Party which rendered the workers' and peasants' councils insignificant.[227]

In November 1920 the anarchist Voline visited Kropotkin and heard from him that the one-party dictatorship in Russia had produced a typical unsuccessful revolution which might lead to a profound reaction.[228] Another visitor in 1920, Vilkens, of the Spanish Confederation of Labor, asked Kropotkin if he wanted to leave Russia. He answered that he wished to die in his beloved Russia. F. De Reyger, a Dutch anarchist, got a letter from Kropotkin at the end of 1920 declining his invitation to live in Holland. He told De Reyger that socialists should be encouraged despite the centralist turn of events in Russia.[229]

Kropotkin died in Dmitrov on February 8, 1921. He had been stricken with pneumonia in January. Lenin had commissioned Bonch-Bruevich to make sure he got all the necessary medical aid when he fell sick. His death notice was put on the front pages of *Izvestia*, *Pravda*, and *Bednota*, and he was hailed by these official organs as a true revolutionary.[230]

Emma Goldman, Alexander Berkman, and Sofia Kropotkin formed a Memorial Committee and applied to the Moscow Soviet for the old Kropotkin house to serve as a museum, which permission was ultimately granted.[231] Nicholas K. Lebedev became its manager.[232] At the end of 1938 the museum was closed down. Sofia had died in early 1938 and Alexandra had emigrated. Peter's only grandchild died as an ambulance nurse in London in 1944.[233]

Today in the Soviet Union a square and a street in Moscow, a small city, a village, and a mountain range bear the name Kropotkin.[234] William Z. Foster, the American Communist party functionary, summed up the official Soviet view of Kropotkin from the vantage point of the 1960s thusly:

He died in the Soviet Union, an honored citizen, but a confirmed opponent of the Bolshevik regime.

He was an enemy of proletarian political parties, of political action, and of the dictatorship of the proletariat. To him the main enemy was the state, not the capitalist class.[235]

CHAPTER 2

Kropotkin within the Anarchist Tradition

T HE anarchist political current is a rich and varied one, and, viewed from the perspective of today's world, it is still a living and relevant viewpoint. The political disestablishment is littered with the vestiges of classical anarchist ideas unreconstructed or more often transformed into vaguely new leftist or generally counterculturist terms and institutions. Typical of the latter phenomenon are such ideas as "back to the land," "worker's control," "direct action," "communes," "small is beautiful," and the general antipolitics mentality.

Kropotkin, by scholarly consensus, belongs to the inner core of anarchist theoreticians. Most students of anarchism acclaim him as the greatest anarchist theoretician, and even among the minority who dispute this it is readily acknowledged that he is second only to Bakunin. What follows will be an attempt to place Kropotkin's intellectual contribution to the anarchist cause within the context of the historical, formative development of anarchist theory, which is essentially a nineteenth–century phenomenon. The primary thrust will be to contrast the contribution of Kropotkin with those of his major anarchist intellectual antecedents and contemporaries and, secondarily, with subsequent anarchist thinkers and actors. But before proceeding to this task, let us examine the intellectual phenomenon called anarchism.

The giants of anarchist thought, seen chronologically, include William Godwin, Max Stirner, Pierre-Joseph Proudhon, Michael Bakunin, and Peter Kropotkin. One might well argue that with Kropotkin's formulation of "anarchist-communism," classical anarchism had received its capstone. It had, through the efforts of these thinkers, developed individualist, mutualist, and collec-

57

tivist variants. The anarcho-communist variant would become
the predominant one, rivaled only by subsequently developed
anarcho-syndicalism. Kropotkin enthusiastically embraced the
anarcho-syndicalist idea, considering it in theory wholly compatible with anarchist-communism. The concept of
anarcho-syndicalism, which is the direct organizational precursor of workers' control, seems to have been the last major form
evolved by classical anarchism.

I   *Toward a Definition*

Before delving into the distinctions between the individualist,
collectivist-mutual, communist and syndicalist variants, and the
men who are identified with these distinctions, let us examine
the nature of anarchism itself as a political ideology. It is a theory
that holds that all forms of government are both wrong and
unnecessary, wrong in the sense that they offend against the
natural autonomy of man and unnecessary in that they are not
needed because man's natural autonomy flows out of his natural
goodness. Hence anarchism asserts that man is basically good and
naturally capable of self-control and self-regulation. Anarchism
aims at excluding all forms of external authority over individuals,
leaving it up to individual initiative to assume freely whatever
degree of cooperation individuals desire in their mutual relations. This extreme individualism is mitigated by the belief that
man is naturally a social animal and hence unfettering the
individual will not dissolve communities although it might
dissolve all extracommunal political associations.

According to Kropotkin, anarchism is a theory of life and
conduct under which society is conceived without government
and in which social harmony is obtained without authoritative
laws or leaders by free agreements concluded between various
groups, territorial or professional, freely constituted for the sake
of production and consumption as well as for the satisfaction of
the infinite variety of needs and aspirations of a civilized being.[1]

Anarchos, the classical Greek word, means "without a ruler,"
and not chaos, as many have assumed because a state-less,
authority-less society has been assumed by those uncongenial to
the anarchist persuasion to be inevitably chaotic. It was first used
as a word of condemnation in the French Revolution, and Pierre-
Joseph Proudhon was apparently the first political theorist

willing to chance the title of anarchist.[2] Anarchists of course do
not accept the equation of anarchy with chaos. As Herbert Read
insists, to be without rulers, which is what anarchism means, is
not to be without order.[3] But the order desired by anarchists is
different from the order imposed by national governments. As
Howard Zinn expresses this:

> They [the anarchists] want a voluntary forming of human relations,
> arising out of the needs of people. Such an order comes from within,
> and so is natural. People flow into easy arrangements, rather than being
> pushed and forced.[4]

The concepts of individual liberty, self-activity, and non-
hierarchical forms of organization have been identified by Paul
Berman as the very basis of anarchism.[5] The individual is the
anarchist's center of society and the freedom of the individual is
the touchstone of progress for them.[6] Yet, while the libertarian
imperative is posed in individual terms, most anarchists, believes
Robert Hoffman, are primarily concerned with the realization of
a just and integral society rather than with individual liberty.[7]
Man is naturally a social animal, the tendency having emerged
with man as he evolved out of the animal world. Society is the
natural milieu of man and is seen as a natural, growing matrix.
Society is the natural construct and manmade laws and
institutions the unnatural. Customs and habits of men which
merged before formal government are considered to be natural
and hence valid. The only authority that is legitimate is natural
authority which emerges from experience and which requires no
coercion for its acceptance. This emphasis on the natural and
prehuman origin of societies has made, says Woodcock, every
anarchist theoretician reject Rousseau's idea of a social contract.
It also makes anarchists reject the notion of any Utopia, since this
implies the achievement of a state of perfection which in turn
implies cessation of growth.[8]

II   *Anarchism and Marxism*

It might be well to compare and contrast the anarchist or
libertarian branch of socialism with the Marxian or so-called
authoritarian branch. According to David Apter: "The virtue of
anarchism as a doctrine is that it employs a socialist critique of

capitalism and a liberal critique of socialism."[9]

Noam Chomsky quotes the anarchist writer Rudolf Rocker to the effect that anarchism represents the attempt to salvage classical liberal ideals wrecked on the reality of capitalist economic forces. Anarchism, according to Rocker, is necessarily anticapitalist in that it opposes the exploitation of man by man but it also opposes the domination of man by man and insists that socialism be free.[10] In its insistence on a revolution from below and its rejection of the "dictatorship of the proletariat" even as a transitional mode, it clearly contrasts with the Marxism of the late nineteenth century, not to speak of the state socialism of the twentieth. In its opposition to any form of coercion, which is epitomized in the modern state and the rule of political parties, it could hardly accommodate to a Marxian or workers' state. The difference over fundamentals was only partially reflected in the famous duel between Bakunin and Marx for control of the First International within which anarchism was the dominant tendency for a number of years. Perhaps a goodly part of the cause for the break between Marxists and anarchists at that time was a matter of the conflict of personalities and ambitions of Marx and Bakunin. But differences of principle cannot be overlooked. If not at that moment then at some point these bedrock differences would have emerged. As Irving L. Horowitz puts it:

> It is shallow to say that the difference between anarchists and socialists is tactical, i.e., that socialists would postpone the abolition of the state while the anarchists want to abolish the state now. What underlies this tactical difference are contrasting theories of human nature.[11]

Horowitz talks of an asceticism intrinsic to anarchism, an addiction to "natural" values and "fundamental" living conditions, a simple belief that all material as well as spiritual needs can be satisfied once the natural laws of society shed the impediments of civilization. Horowitz attributes the absence of a well-worked-out commitment to economic development in the anarchist theory to this attitude.[12] Obviously Marxism supplies a thorough theoretical construct for economic analysis, and one which requires tremendous centralization of production with a coordination based on a high degree of integration and which implied a progressive homogenization of the fabric of society from the top down.

Whatever the true status of Marxian economic "laws," the very word rings abhorrent to anarchist ears. Anarchism proceeds not from economic analysis but from a moral imperative: from the Kantian ethic that the only true morality is one in which there would be no longer a distinction between what is done for one's self and what is done for others.[13] Kropotkin devoted great efforts in attempting to ground the anarchist moral imperative in the bedrock of science, much in the same way that Engels attempted to verify Marx's historical materialism by reference to the laws of dialectical materialism which he claimed to have derived from the natural sciences. But regardless of the parallel convocation of the God of science to buttress their claims, the anarchists, including Kropotkin, were comfortable with the very concept of ethics and morality whereas for the Marxists this is a wholly fallacious category, a superstructural blind. For the anarchists there was a realm of absolute human values whereas for the Marxists morality was class determined and a dependent rather than an independent variable in the dynamics of social change.

But the anarchist imperative of freedom from coercion dictates that morality not be defined in terms of a set of obligatory strictures. Instead, Krimerman and Perry note, anarchism stresses the state of character underlying and expressed by any moral decision, holding such uncoerced ethical behavior to be the dynamics of human improvement.[14]

Anarchism and Marxism differ fundamentally in the attitudes toward nature. Anarchism views the relation between man and nature as essentially one of harmony, not opposition. As Marshal Shatz puts it:

> Human society is not a collective enterprise for the mastery of nature but an organic outgrowth of nature, and the ills of society stem from efforts to impose artificial constraints on its free, spontaneous development.[15]

For the anarchist nature was not "dumb." It was not merely the raw material out of which man the worker fashions civilization. Nature was seen as spontaneous, unpatterned creativity. The anarchists extol the virtue of spontaneity and felt a strong affinity with the peasantry, whereas Marx dismissed the idiocy of rural life and proclaimed the goal of transforming rural labor into a variety of industrial labor through collectivizing agricultural production, introducing factories into the countryside, and overcoming the gulf between the urban and rural ways of life. The proletariat is declared the most progressive class, and its leadership proclaimed within the party and during and after the revolution. Marxists have often regarded the peasant as at best an unreliable ally whose fate it was to be transformed into a worker. Yet Marx, in the fact of Bakunin's criticisms, did disavow any intention of coercing the peasantry into collective labor and called for a postrevolutionary policy which would bring the peasantry immediate benefits and thereby win them over to collective property.

The anarchists were not rejecting modern industry and technology. They were not Luddites or uncritical romantic worshipers of nature. Rather they saw in the growth of industry and technology forces which were progressively dehumanizing more and more people and uprooting what they considered to be healthier life-styles such as those of craftsmen, artisans, and petty farmers. The assembly line was reducing the worker to being an appendage of the machine. It was destroying much of the aesthetic and spiritual mode of expression. It was despoiling the landscape and creating ugly urban agglomerations. For the anarchist work was primarily an expression of the creative personality of the individual, a view which the young Marx reflected. But for the mature Marx work was a means to the end of ever increasing productivity and efficiency, and nature was merely the raw material of work. Ultimately, of course, once a superabundance of goods was available, traditional work and the state would disappear.

Moreover, the anarchists saw the small community as the ideal environment for the free play of man's personality. Personal relationships were more feasible in this environment. Anarchists insisted on the decentralization of life and the simplification of social relations. They emphasized the need for direct control by the worker over his world conditions and over all aspects of his life. Self-government became more difficult to attain the more complex the work or living environment was. While anarchists like Kropotkin were not oblivious to the benefits of large-scale production, they insisted that maximal production and efficiency were false gods. Kropotkin himself undertook to demonstrate the reconcilability of small-scale production, progressive technology, and a superabundance of goods. Many of his fellow anarchists were willing to sacrifice some of the advantages of advanced industrial civilization—not all, by any means—in order to restore human proportions. The anarchists were most faithful to the problems of alienation so well described by the "young Marx," and they retained the highest priority on the anarchist agenda.

To the Marxist the anarchist commendation of the small communities of the past, usually agrarian, seems reactionary, uncritical, and certainly ascientific. It smacks of romanticism and populism. Marxists refuse to accord virtue to those who live lives that are simpler and closer to nature's rhythms. What is more natural is not necessarily any better or more virtuous. And while most anarchists, as noted above, are not against the benefits of industrialization, they are very anxious about the trends implicit in rapid and relentless industrialization, anxieties not often shared by Marxist political parties.

For the Marxist progress is seen in terms of furthering the complexity of society and the economy and in greater productivity and production. For the anarchist, according to Woodcock, progress

> implies not progress in terms of society as it now exists, but rather retreat along the lines of simplification, a rebellion not necessarily in favor of the past but in favor of an ideal of individual freedom which belongs outside the present in which they find themselves. [16]

Progress lies with the abolition of authority and the progressive reclaiming of the necessary leisure which would allow the cultivation of the mind and spirit, a return to a condition of life in which, as Woodcock puts it, the natural processes resume their influence over the lives of societies and individuals.[17] For the Marxist, anarchism provides no method or power for maintaining the economic productivity that generates this leisure and the abundance anarchism assumes, a criticism shared with non-Marxian commentators.

Anarchism and Marxism share a fundamental antipathy to capitalism and a commitment to transcending it by a combination of revolution and evolution, depending on times and circumstances. Both are revolutionary credos. But to the anarchist revolution is a moral necessity rather than an historically inevitable event.[18] The anarchists reject outright the Marxian laws of historical materialism. They reject the notion of ironclad

historical laws at work within human society pushing history in
one direction. Men with the necessary information can prevent
the fulfillment of any social prediction. Any man can free himself
from the bounds of social culpability:

> All behavior can be self-governing and individualized. To the
> objection that individualized self-deceptivity ignores the statistical
> control of social laws, the anarchist replies that a generalization about
> behavior is not necessarily an explanatory law.[19]

Both anarchists and Marxists are willing to accept violence as a
legitimate means to anticapitalist revolution. But the organizational approach to revolution, not to speak here of the
postrevolutionary organization of society, creates a fundamental
divergence reflective of differing philosophical values. In a
fundamental sense anarchists are antipolitical. Politics and the
state mechanism are the realm of coercion. Revolution is
justified, as are revolutionary force and violence, only to
establish a coercion-free society of voluntary institutions. A
political party is inherently a restrictive device and creates a
privileged group of members. Anarchists reject political action
per se as inherently tainted with the fungus of power lust. Unlike
the Marxists, they refuse to countenance a transitional statist
society in the name of the largest single class, the proletariat, as a
dictatorship over the rest of society until the requisite economic
and cultural revolution frees society from the chains of scarcity
and selfishness. Anarchists have generally attacked any well-
meaning attempts to play the parliamentary game as fundamentally compromising. Anything that binds the individual to the will
of others is rejected. Hence anarchism opposes parliamentary
democracy and holds that only the sovereignty of the individual
is valid. Representative government and rule by democratically
elected majorities, not to speak of coups by revolutionary
minorities, are all rejected. As Woodcock puts it, for the
anarchist right lies not in numbers but in reason.[20] And, as
Kropotkin reiterated, the end cannot justify the means. Rather
the means can pervert the end.
    Implicit in the anarchist value of individual autonomy in all
spheres of life is the notion of workers' control. It is just a
particular case of the general direct democracy in the gover-
nance of all matters of mutual interest and mutual cooperation
which is for anarchists the only method of conduct of public

affairs consonant with the social autonomy of the individual. It is the same workers' control that emerged in Soviet Russia in the period of 1917 to 1921 and in theory exists in significant sectors of the Yugoslav and Chinese systems as well as in the communes of the counterculture. It was one of the banners of the 1968 revolt in France. More to the point, "workers' control" blossomed into the anarcho-syndicalist idea in the late nineteenth century. According to Berman, the local assemblies, the free associations of individuals for mutual aid, and collective action are "the critical institutions of anarchy":

Freely generated and disbanded, such assemblies are a full and direct democracy, reaching decisions by consensus and free experimentation but not by the tyranny of the majority. The basic economic organization is the workers' council, the local assembly in the fields as in the factory, shop, and store. Similarly, neighborhood and local political and social groupings would form communes administered by free assemblies. Totally accountable and instantly recallable delegates would unite the various councils and communes into a series of broader federations—industrial, agricultural, regional, and national. The federations would aid, share, coordinate, and even economically centralize, but they would have no existence outside the local assemblies, nor would there be any form of political centralism; the right of secession is paramount and indisputable. Power would remain decentralized in each council and commune.[21]

Since the anarchists reject the delegation of power and hence political representatives, "the freedom of self-management exists only where it is self-gained, self-proclaimed, and self-maintained."[22] Anarchists among the workers do not form a leadership caste or group. Rather they help, urge, and reform.[23] They are not privileged by virtue of their insights. They are catalytic agents and not manipulators. Revolutionary consciousness must penetrate the masses through the self-realization of the individual. The anarchists reject any form of Leninist compulsory tutelage. They insist on revolution from below, spontaneity rather than consciousness in its Leninist sense.

A final point of contrast between anarchism and Marxism is in order before proceeding to a discussion of the major historical schools of anarchism. While the Marxist concept of internationalism is hardly free of important, perhaps even crucial ambiguities, the anarchist concept borders on invisibility. The anarchists, primarily under Bakunin, did play for some years a major role in the First International. And they subsequently indulged in the creation of anarchist internationals. But as for positing some international organization of society or a postrevolutionary international order, they left it to implication. Presumably the notion of free communes and federations of free communes on the national level would simply be extended to the international level. But what about the future of nationalities and nations? The only guide was the principle of the equality and the freedom of all. Anarchism tended to ignore the concrete and topical problems of suffering nationalities in favor of a vague commitment to federalism. Since it saw freedom and liberty in individual terms, it was somewhat insensitive to the needs of national groups for corporate self-determination. There is virtually no theoretical account taken of the notion of nationalities, their aspirations to self-determination, and the economic implications or viability of such would-be nations. Cognate questions like the linguistic problems of national minorities or problems of defining a nationality were virtually ignored. Such problems were left for such times as they became compelling. They were not seen as primary and could be left for improvisation in the event of the situation. This was in essence true to the deep-seated anarchist value of spontaneity, of not imposing on life a stenciled, hence artificial, rigid solution. Let those concerned decide for themselves.

The intention in what follows is to compare Kropotkin's major contribution to anarchist thought with those other major formulators of anarchist doctrine who preceded him. This is not a comprehensive survey of all significant anarchist thinkers but rather a study of those few generally conceded to be the major innovators. The scope is limited to characterizing their most distinctive contributions to the foundation of theoretical anarchism rather than dwelling on the nuances and discreet distinctions of emphasis and detail which separate them. Moreover, it is my belief, and that of most students of anarchism, that virtually no anarchist thinkers after Kropotkin rank with these major figures. The approach will be strictly chronological.

III   The Earliest Anarchist Theorist: William Godwin

William Godwin (1756-1836) first published his only major work, *Enquiry Concerning Political Justice, and Its Influence on*

Morals and Happiness, in 1793. Godwin was an ex-Presbyterian minister who had given up the ministry in 1783 and some four years later had become an atheist. *The Enquiry* became the bible of modern anarchism. Its main tenets which left their mark on all subsequent anarchist theoreticians were: man is a child of reason and in the cultivation and perfection of reason lies virtue and happiness; man is amenable to rational persuasion and he can overcome environmental factors as well as emotional; society is nothing more than an aggregation of individuals and that which is good for individuals is good for society; man must cultivate his own reason and no external authority or institution can or should force him to see reason.

Godwin believes government was intended to suppress injustice but instead embodies and perpetuates it. It concentrates the force of the community and conducts world projects, wars, and in general oppresses. By perpetuating and aggravating the inequality of property, it incites the passions which lead to robbery and fraud. Government's means is restriction, an abridgment of individual independence. Happiness for man requires independence. Consequently, the most desirable state of mankind is that which maintains general society, with the smallest encroachment upon individual independence.[24] Since government inherently involves force and since force is inimical to reason, all government is an evil; democracy, the least evil form of government, is still an appeal to numbers, not reason; men must be free from all constraints except those of reason and argument; all men are entitled to the necessities of life; but the injustice of accumulated property, which divides men into rich and poor, giving rise to crime, wars, envy, and dissipation, should be removed; the freest society would be one in which needs were few and simple, and each man had his own means of meeting these needs.

Reason requires that no man try by force to correct inequality in property. Reason would probably, in a well-ordered community, be sufficient to restrain men from this. Accumulation in the simple society would be restrained by the good sense of the community. As to inheritance, there is no merit involved in being born to a rich man.[25] The society which best achieves simplicity would have to be a decentralized confederacy of small, independent local groups; centralized states are harmful since they trade upon a fictitious national pride and distribute privileges and property; individual reason, not a legislature, should be the sole legislator.

Godwin's view of human nature and society remains central to all subsequent anarchist thought: man associated at first for the sake of mutual assistance. "Society is produced by our wants, and government by our wickedness."[26] The wise man is activated by neither ambition nor interest and knows no jealousy. He must be guided only by the dictates of reason.

While the triumph of truth is certain, it is for Godwin a gradual process and reason alone is the only weapon to use in the fight against error. Resort to force is precluded, because force cannot be a substitute for reason even if enlisted on the side of reason. And thus government, which is coercion, must be eliminated. Positive institutions, Godwin's name for government, cannot inform one's understanding because truth is recognized by one's understanding and not from the statement of authority.[27] Atendranath Bose notes that Godwin's faith in the invincibility of truth is unshakable and unqualified.[28] He is an extreme individualist, disliking cooperation as detrimental to individual freedom except in such forms as scientific research, conversation, etc.[29] Godwin's Utopia is a society of equals without privileges or property beyond that which serves to satisfy simple needs. The revolution in his opinion will introduce a liberal approach toward property and gradually reduce accumulation. Gradually institutions and governments will disappear without the use of force but through rational criticism. As Isaac Kramnick notes, Godwin is no revolutionary. He assumes the ultimate victory of anarchism as ignorance retreats before advancing enlightenment.[30]

Irving L. Horwitz labels the first conscious form of anarchism "utilitarian anarchism." It represents a compound of nostalgia and utopianism developed by an enlightened sector of the aristocracy, an expression by the déclassé wealthy on behalf of the underprivileged. Out of a need for guilt alleviation, a Helvetius, Diderot, and a Godwin appeal to reason to manufacture reasonable creatures from below while appealing to rational authorities from above. Their assumption was that knowledge and truth could overcome ignorance and interests.[31] Horowitz also notes that Godwin ignores economics.[32] Kropotkin was by far the most sophisticated economist among the major anarchist theoreticians, and he certainly did not share Godwin's distaste for cooperation which he made the cornerstone of his economic prescriptions. Moreover, Godwin, like Hobbes, his philosophical enemy, assumed that social analysis starts with the individual, his personal needs and desires, rather than with society's or the state's. As April Carter puts it, for both Hobbes and Godwin, human nature is seen as more fundamental than any specific social or cultural influence.[33] Kropotkin, in attempting to combat the Hobbesian notion of the state as a necessary evil in order to check the aggressive nature of individuals, evokes "society" as a repository of cooperation and altruism in contrast to the inherently evil state.[34] Hence Kropotkin evokes "society" as an alternative to the state, an alternative not provided by Godwin's extreme individualism. And Kropotkin also attempts to adduce biological and historical proof for the Godwinian *ex cathedra* statement that human beings are essentially rational. Still, like Godwin, Kropotkin too uncritically accepts the idea of an active public opinion as an easy way out of the problem of dealing with antisocial tendencies. According to Woodcock:

> Few of them (the anarchists) have given sufficient thought to the danger of a moral tyranny replacing a physical one, and the frown of the man next door becoming a thing to fear as the sentence of the judge.[35]

What emerges from Godwin's first great anarchist treatise as a legacy to the future movement is an emphasis on the rational nature of men, their natural tendency toward virtue, the notion of progress as a process of moral perfection, the idea that coercion in general and government as its most characteristic form are evil, and that the virtuous life is one based on simple tastes and pursuits requiring only a minimal amount of property to supply necessities, and a highly decentralized form of society. What is missing is any empirical underpinnings or historical evidence for his views of human nature, or any theory of how to guide the economic interactions and production activities of his exceedingly small series of local communities.

IV   *Anarchism's First Mature Formulator:*
Pierre-Joseph Proudhon

With Pierre-Joseph Proudhon (1809–1865) we first encounter an anarchist theoretician of the first order who is actively

involved in revolutionary activities. Proudhon was at first wholly
a peasant radical. One biographer notes that *What Is Property?*
(1840) seemed to take into account only the farmer and the
handicraftsman. But by 1848 his contacts with the Lyons
weavers had made him conscious of the need for cooperation.
His vision of the People's Bank was based on the idea of
association for the exchange of products between peasants and
small workshop groups. Subsequent industrialism convinced him
of the need to create closely knit productive associations of
workers in certain trades. Finally, in the 1860s, he appealed to
the factory workers.[36] Proudhon reflects Godwin in attacking
hierarchical centralization of the state as the oppressor of
people. But he is far more the socialist than Godwin. True
socialism is based on justice, and justice consists of striking a
balance between freedom of the individual, and unity of order.
The structural form he hits upon for reconciling these is
federalism. Proudhon expresses what would become—Godwin
having already enunciated it—the fundamental anarchist premise that men are most free in small, simple communities. But as
Marshall Shatz notes, he added a significant new element to
anarchist theory by viewing these small communities, where
voluntary assent to life-affecting decisions was alone feasible, as
primarily economic associations. Proudhon's society is engen-
dered by that long-loved creature of the Enlightenment, *homo
economicus.*[37]

Proudhon was the first anarchist theoretician to supply a
fundamental critique of Marx's communism, a critique which
influenced Bakunin and Kropotkin. Proudhon could be said to
have given anarchism its anti-Marxian strain. He was also the first
serious anarchist student of economic man and he backed his
federalist substitute for centralist states with an economic idea
known as mutualism. Proudhon tried to link the economic
restructuring of society with the political.

In yet another sense Proudhon is more the socialist than
Godwin. His basic thought is not individualistic. For the mature
Proudhon, despite his tolerance of individual peasant property,
what is opposed to the state "is not the individual as such but the
individual in organic connection with his group, the group being
a voluntary association of individuals." Proudhon's anticentralism
became, progressively, communalism and federalism.[38] This
concern with society as the starting point for social analysis, the

major analytical category, becomes the dominant anarchist approach with the exception of that of the anarchist individualist school.

Before delving into the major tenets of Proudhon's thought, one must note that there are some very specific links between Proudhon and Kropotkin on the level of ideas. First of all, Proudhon's analysis of property with its famous conclusion that property is theft, and the derivative conclusion that differences in income are generally not justified, will be espoused by Kropotkin. These inferences were meant to apply especially to industrial labor, since according to Proudhon all production is collective in a large industrial society with division of labor. Therefore, the product belongs to society. Productive capacity itself is a social creation. And in many cases, not just industrial, the means of production are uncreated by man.[39] There is no doubt that Kropotkin drew upon Proudhon in fashioning his own analysis of the injustice of the property and wage systems, an analysis whose conclusions were far more egalitarian and thoroughly communistic than Proudhon's.

A second specific link is Proudhon's idea of integrated education, with instruction inseparable from apprenticeship and scientific education inseparable from professional education. A third Proudhonian seed which Kropotkin sowed was the former's idea of the possibility due to new technology — this was written in 1855 — of making the concentration of population in big cities unnecessary and gradually shifting the political center of gravity to new agricultural and industrial groupings outside the cities.[40] Kropotkin developed the notion of technology making small-scale industry feasible and more dispersable so that urban agglomeration could be contained and even thinned out. Kropotkin would become the major proponent of integrated education, embellishing and developing this Proudhonian theme parenthetically introduced into symphonic form.

Like Proudhon, Kropotkin condemned luxury. Work was a virtue, idleness a vice. But unlike Kropotkin, Proudhon had no faith in industrialization as the deliverer of mankind. He scorned any doctrine of automatic progress. He only hoped for a social order which would hold man's evil tendencies in check, not bring about the millennium. Nor did Proudhon share Kropotkin's rage for complete equality. His ideal was the mean. The industrious should be rewarded proportionately more than the lazy, although differences in reward should never become great enough to produce extremes of wealth and power. Proudhon, like Godwin, held that if men limited their needs to those of the simple life of the land, then nature would provide enough for all. Commerce was a cosmopolitan evil.[41] Again, unlike Kropotkin, Proudhon did not accept the necessity for class hostility. His socialism was rather an alliance of the lesser bourgeoisie, the industrial workers and the peasants against the growing wealth of the capitalists. He defended the small-property owner, and his "property is theft" meant only that those who owned land without working it were thieves. Proudhon not only believed in the exclusive individual possession of landed property limited only in size but conceived of cooperation as operative only between independent producers. Kropotkin did not accept exclusive possession of land and had a concept of cooperation involving joint production. Proudhon opposed common ownership of land and defended hereditary property as one of the foundations of the family and of society. Kropotkin totally rejected inheritance.[42]

For Proudhon, every man, from the fact of his existence, has the right to occupy land and to cultivate it, not to own it. And society oversees this. Thus there is absolute equality in the right of occupancy, with size determined by numbers and social conditions. Society grants use of the land and society alone is permanent possessor.[43] The worker has an absolute right to what he produces but not to raw materials provided by nature. His product is social because the heritage of installations and techniques is a product of mankind collectively. Proudhon's most serious objection to property in the means of production is that to accept it is to destroy equality.[44] It creates a monopoly. It gives the owner income for which he has not worked. Labor alone is productive. Land or capital does not produce.[45] It creates a monopoly. The laborer must get all of the fruits of his labor, and although this will also create inequality it is not so fearful because there is a limit on the amount of goods producible by one worker.[46] Proudhon wants products and skills of diverse power to be exchanged on equal terms. He wants an equilibrium to attain in free exchange. Proudhon is not against property *per se*, but only against its abuse, against an imbalance in its distribution. He sees in the right of workers freely to dispose of their products and keep their savings the very essence of liberty.[47] Products will be exchanged for others of the same value. But no word on how or why this should be.

Proudhon attacks socialists for favoring compulsory associations. The latter he considers slavery. While property begets inequality, communism begets slavery. A balance is needed. Property and the liberty of work and exchange must be preserved. But the claim to unearned income will be suppressed by limiting property to the fruits of one's own labor. Proudhon looks for a social system free of privileges and monopolies in which each party to an exchange would receive value equal to what he gave. This system he calls mutualism. Goods will be exchanged at equal value and profit eliminated. The new society is based on free associations which will maintain equality in the means of production and equivalence of exchange. To this end an exchange bank will be created in order to give free credit to the producer. It will issue bills of credit which will be given for the client's goods and circulate like money. It will control and fix the prices of goods based on an assessment of the labor and expenses of production.[48]

Proudhon felt that through the bank a network of independent craftsmen and peasants and associations of workers could be created who would contract out of the capitalist system and eventually achieve a peaceful transformation of society. Thus Proudhon accepts the need for large-scale industry, while retaining an independent peasantry and small family workshops. He also accepts competition between producers. The middleman is to be eliminated.[49] Transformation would come through convincing society of the justice of the order. The mutualist idea must win general acceptance. Reason, not force, is the means.[50] Proudhon, in correspondence with Marx, opposed revolutionary action as an appeal to force.[51] Liberation would come only through the widespread acceptance of fundamental economic action. The economic transformation underlies and is prior to the political. But for Proudhon economic action is not precipitate or incendiary. On this essential Proudhon parts company with Bakunin and Kropotkin and seems to cling to Godwin's non-revolutionary road to the transformation of society.

It is in the generalization of the principle of contract, that is a voluntary mode of understanding between free individuals or groups, that Proudhon sees the new society. Contract will replace government, each town or industrial union will make its own laws. Workers will run their enterprises, and courts will be replaced by arbitration processes. In his book *On the Federal Principle* (1863) he saw federation as a stage on the way to anarchy. The organization of administration should begin locally as near to the direct control of the people as possible. Above this primary level the confederal organization would become less an organ of administration than of coordination between local primary units. Thus the nation would be replaced by a geographical confederation of regions, which themselves are voluntary clusters of communes, and Europe would become a confederation of confederations, in which the interests of the smallest province would have as much voice as the largest, and in which all affairs would be settled by mutual agreement, contract, and arbitration.[52]

While Proudhon was an ardent believer in decentralization economically and politically, he saw the tide of the time running toward greater centralization, even among socialists, especially Marxists. Kropotkin some four to five decades later was quite optimistic about the strong evidence of accelerating decentralization in economic and social life. On this point certainly Proudhon's pessimism proved more realistic than Kropotkin's optimism.

And while both Proudhon and Kropotkin favored voluntary cooperation in production, Proudhon felt that it was far more appropriate to the industrial sphere than to the agricultural. In general Proudhon gave far narrower scope to cooperation than Kropotkin, who did not see any sphere as inappropriate to a far more thorough type of cooperative mechanism than Proudhon's. And of course Kropotkin's communism with its distribution according to need transcended Proudhon's mutualism, with its seemingly incongruous free market and competition between groups and individuals.

V   Max Stirner: Precursor of Individualist Anarchism

Max Stirner (1806-1856) represents the most extreme representative of the unfettered ego or ultraindividualist current in anarchism. He waged war on all the extraindividual abstractions which prevented the individual from venting fully his egoistic strivings. His only major work, *The Ego and His Own* (1845), is a classic of anarchist thought and influenced the American school of individualist anarchists which included Benjamin Tucker, Josiah Warren, and Lysander Spooner. This school is distinguished by its view of the ego or individual as the center of sensitivity and consciousness. The individual must be accorded priority, and the social dichotomy is framed in terms of the individual versus the state, which oppresses the individual. Irving Horowitz detects six defining characteristics of this school of thought: first, a belief that a collective society in any form is impossible without leading to an authoritarian system. This leads to the defense of private property or individual proprietorship, as long as it involves only the fruit of one's own labor. Second, the purpose of society is held to be the preservation of the sovereignty of every individual, hence all associations based on limiting this individual sovereignty, particularly the state, must be curbed and eventually eliminated. Third, the principle of mutualism is to be arrived at on a voluntary basis and by withdrawal from the involuntary statist institutions. Fourth, the principle of equality requires racial, sexual, and labor equality. Anarchism thus must seek the extinction of interest, rent, dividends, profits, except as represented by work done. Fifth, majority rule is unacceptable as an infringement upon the natural rights of the individual. No rightful authority can be external to individual consent, hence all such authority legitimizes civil disobedience, resistance, and even destruction. Sixth, any definition of liberty begins and concludes with the liberty of the weaker party in a nation. The free and basic test of liberty is the right to disobey majority legislation.[53]

There are overtones of the nihilist in Stirner which suggest that he influenced Bakunin. There is also in his super egoism something that recommends him as a precursor of Nietzsche. Stirner attacks the state as the tyrant bending individual wills to its own. Its only purpose is to subordinate the individual with its violence which it calls law.[54] Truth, right, morality, love, and justice are all specters of a crazy mind. Right is nothing more than the privilege of superior power. Only from egoism, not love of others, states Stirner, can the poor obtain property:

> Thousands of years of civilization have obscured to you what you are, have made you believe you are not egoists but are called to be idealists ("good men"). Shake that off! Do not seek for freedom, which does precisely deprive you of yourselves, in self-denial; but seek for yourselves, become egoists, become each of you an almighty ego.[55]

The earth belongs to those who know how to take it.[56] Stirner's ideal egoist is the individual who does not shrink from the use of any means in the war of each against all, who judges everything ruthlessly from the viewpoint of his own well-being and may enter with like-minded individuals into a union of egoists without rules or regulations, for the pursuit of common interests and only for as long as these last.[57]

Morality is incompatible with egoism because it does not allow validity to me. The state and I are enemies, declares Stirner:

> I, the egoist, have not at heart the welfare of this human society, I sacrifice nothing to it, I only utilize it; but to be able to utilize it completely I transform it rather into my property and my creature; that is, I annihilate it, and form in its place the nation of egoists.[58]

All egoists are equal because each individual is unique, and the only duty is to cultivate that uniqueness. One's ego is the only law. The state, whether despotic or democratic, is the negation of individual will. Stirner's only attempt to explain how a social equilibrium might ensue in this constant warfare is his belief that self-realization does not require burdening oneself with more possessions than one requires, and that to rule over others destroys one's own independence. Woodcock rightly concludes that Stirner opposes society as well as the state, since it too is based on a collectivist conception of man.[59] All methods are acceptable for the poor to use in order to take from the rich.[60] Stirner, then, is uncompromising in his insistence that the only form of government is the self-government of the ego. And yet Stirner could not conceive of the ego existing outside society. There is no suggestion that a retreat from society is possible.

VI   Russian Anarchism: Herzen and Bakunin

Russian anarchism, of which Michael Bakunin was the first full-blown political representative, had its beginnings in both the Christian quietism of Leo Tolstoi and his followers and the Petrashevsky circle in St. Petersburg, which transmitted Fourier's utopian socialism to Russia during the 1840s. While revolutionary anarchists could not accept Tolstoi's doctrine of nonresistance to evil, they could embrace his antistate, antiwar, antipatriotic communitarianism coupled with his deep compassion for the unspoiled peasantry. The Russian Slavophiles of the mid-nineteenth century also held the centralized, bureaucratic state to be an unmitigated evil.[61]

Alexander Herzen, one of the intellectual fathers of Russian socialism and its most characteristic progeny, populism, was also a very strong initial influence on Bakunin and the young Kropotkin. Herzen, the illegitimate but well provided for son of a Russian nobleman, formulated a notion of Russia as a younger, more hopeful society from the standpoint of revolutionary potential than Western Europe. He had come to feel in the late 1840s that both the educated minority of the gentry, which had demonstrated its disillusionment in the Decembrist uprising of 1825, and the utterly alienated and downtrodden peasantry, were the uncompromising foes of the brutal autocracy. Herzen held than the Russian state was not really Russian at all. He contrasted it with the Slavophile notion of the primitive democracy and socialism of its peasant commune. The Russian state was unnatural, the peasant commune natural. Only the pressure of external enemies—the Mongols, Poles, etc.—made it necessary. The commune, for all its distortion over the centuries, husbanded the spirit of Slav distrust for authority and love of free association. This Russian or Slavic peasant commune involved informalized customary law, free cooperation of equals, and periodic redistribution of commune land so as to preclude any idea of private property.[62]

Yet Martin Malia notes that Herzen's ideal commune did not involve communal living or group labor, which in fact did not exist in the Russian peasant commune or *obshchina*. For Herzen, each commune household would be a separate economic unit, and the commune itself would be largely an association of independent peasant producers. This was, as Malia opines, much closer to Proudhon's mutualist Utopia of individualistic small-holders, each possessing his own plot. Herzen idealized the commune not for its "mutualist" ownership of land but rather for its embodiment of Herzen's anarchist principle of the voluntary association of equals. For Herzen it was a means for fostering the development of individuality. Socialism would result from the fusion of the democratic equality of the Russian commune with the Western principle of the dignity of the individual.[63] Moreover, Herzen, while holding that in Russia the future depended on the peasant, believed that a revolutionary gentry was utterly essential to the success of the revolution.[64]

Herzen made no claim that his theory of revolution was scientific. In fact he did not even call explicitly for a mass uprising. He placed his principle hope for regeneration in the enlightened minority. Thus, while his end—a federation of socialist communes—was radical, his means—a gradualist change from above—were hardly so.[65] Yet as of 1865 Herzen's place in the spectrum of Russian revolutionary thought was at the extreme left, matched only by Bakunin. Malia feels that the differences between them were, however, quite significant. Herzen was the representative of a positive anarchism, and Bakunin of negative anarchism. Bakunin's sole emphasis was on disorganization and destruction. He hoped for a holocaust. Herzen did not see destruction as an end in itself. His emphasis was on promoting humanitarian sentiment in Russia, advancing education, and advancing civil liberties. His vision of an anarchist federation of communes represented a real effort to imagine how local self-government, individual initiative, and a guaranteed minimum of well-being could be realized quickly in Russian agrarian society. Malia concludes that Herzen's socialism was collectivistic in form but individualistic in content. He was inspired by the democratic ideal, which translated into a Russia in which every individual would enjoy the fullness of life. He had an extraordinarily exalted, individualistic and elitist concept of what the full life was. It involved absolute personal freedom, total egoism, and full consciousness. Socialism for him meant raising the people to a life of civilized refinement, not a return to a state of nature. This is an aesthetic concept of personality and a goal of absolute ethical freedom for the individual. As Malia puts it, this may be characterized as an exclusive preoccupation with the essence of man considered in rarefied abstraction from the concrete social or economic situations in which real men exist.[66]

For Malia, Bakunin's anarchism appeared in comparison as a fantastic game of philosophical negation, conspiracy, and insurrection, conducted for the adolescent delight of applying in a ruthlessly logical way this negation. In fact, Bakunin was the more thoroughgoing anarchist, which character Malia holds against him. To Malia anarchism is an irresponsible doctrine since it places itself outside the political possibilities offered by the real world. Anarchism is less a serious political program than an abstract fantasy of negation; it is quintessential intransigence, pure protest. It is the politics of someone whose politics is above all compounded of his refusals, or who is unable, because of the situation of practical impotence in which he finds himself, to formulate his positive goals except as fantasy.[67]

Nevertheless Bakunin's importance is largely due to his channeling anarchist theory into a program of practical political action. With Bakunin anarchist theory became a theory of practical political action and simultaneously changed from the doctrine of the radical wing of the petty bourgeoisie to that of the mass of workers and even the lumpen proletariat.[68]

Both Michael Bakunin and Peter Kropotkin were born of noble Russian families and both forsook military careers for revolutionary politics. But Bakunin (1814–1876) spent most of his life as an anarchist actively planning, plotting, and indulging in revolutionary adventure or managing anarchist organizations. In fact he was the founder of the historical anarchist movement.[69] As a result he left his major mark on the theory and practice of organizing and planning revolution. And his ideas can be considered the basis upon which anarcho-syndicalism was built. He was a strong believer in the revolutionary act as an assertion of human dignity against the evil of hierarchy, authority, and the stage. His famous line about the urge to destroy being a creative urge was born of an activism in the front line of revolution, experiences which were foreign to Kropotkin. Bakunin's famous battle with Marx within the First International not only influenced Kropotkin's views of Marxism but very probably contributed to his anti-German attitude, an attitude which came to the surface at the outbreak of the First World War. Because of his almost total involvement in the anarchist movement and perhaps because of his impetuous personality, he left no totally finished booklength works. As Marshall Shatz puts it: "Bakunin's writings vividly reflect his personality. They are lively and colorful, but disorganized, impulsive, and completely undisciplined."[70]

Shatz's view reflects that of Bertrand Russell writing some fifty-three years earlier when he described Bakunin's writings as chaotic, topical, abstract, not coming to close quarters with economic facts, mostly metaphysical, and unclear about what his desired society would be like or how it could be preserved. Russell commended Kropotkin's writings as the nearest approach to a finished and systematic body of anarchist doctrine.[71]

Kropotkin's formulation of anarchist-communism represented

an outgrowth or transcendence of the collectivist anarchism usually associated with Bakunin. Kropotkin entered anarchism's ranks in the middle 1870s as a Bakuninist. Only after a debate within the Bakuninist ranks on the issue of the collectivist versus communist approach to remuneration for labor did Kropotkin provide the intellectual rationale and the personal persuasion and advocacy to convert the majority of Bakuninists to what was called anarchist-communism. But Kropotkin built upon the Bakuninist legacy, which included an ideologically heterogeneous and organizationally diverse anarchist movement anchored mostly in the craft and trade union associations of Switzerland and Belgium. The movement, thanks largely to Bakunin, had gone over to the collectivist anarchist view from Proudhonist mutualism although Proudhonians were still uneasily settled within the collectivist majority. Moreover, even the mutualists were, under the relentless revolutionary energy of Bakunin, coming to accept the necessity of outright revolutionary tactics, something Proudhon in late career frowned upon. Thus one must give credit to Bakunin for forging a genuine anarchist monument for the first time and basing it upon a concept which represented a far more formidable challenge to the Marxist doctrine in appealing to the masses in the name of social revolution.

There is another sense in which Bakunin's "collectivist" anarchism can be understood. Irving L. Horowitz uses the term to denote Bakunin's freeing of anarchism from a class base and placing it on a mass base. For Bakunin the concept of the proletariat is more a matter of self-definition than of economic position in the factory system. For the Bakuninists words like "proletariat," "peasantry," "toilers," "people," even "lumpenproletariat," are interchangeable. As Horowitz sees it, "At the core of collectivist anarchism lies the consideration that the state claims as its victim society as a whole, the exploited mass as a whole, and not just any particular class."[72] Therefore socialism's task is a collective one, since communism is a collective need. The anarchist's role is to prevent the state from breaking up the solidarity of the oppressed by unifying them under one banner.[73] And Kropotkin was to further develop the theoretical analysis and argument to support what was for Bakunin primarily an instinctual revolutionary tactic.

Both Marx and Bakunin shared a belief in violent revolution, but Marx saw this revolution as being led by a trained and disciplined class-conscious proletariat whereas Bakunin envisioned a peasant-led spontaneous revolution. Despite his belief in spontaneity Bakunin was the originator of the conception of a select and closely organized revolutionary party, bound by ideals and implicit obedience to an absolute revolutionary dictator, a view Kropotkin spurned.[74]

For Bakunin, man is the most social animal and society is the natural medium of the human collectivity. The state is not a direct product of nature, but society is; its existence precedes the awakening of thought in man and needs no contract for its establishment.[75] Man does not become man, nor does he achieve awareness of his humanity other than in society, and man in isolation can have no awareness of liberty. Being free means being treated as such by another man. Liberty is a feature not of isolation but of interaction, "for the liberty of any individual is nothing more or less than the reflection of his humanity and his human rights in the awareness of all free men—his brothers, his equals."[76]

The liberty of man consists solely in obeying natural laws because he has himself recognized them as such and not because they have been externally imposed upon him by an extrinsic will, divine, human, collective or individual. Bakunin rejects all authority, all legislation and all privileged official and legal influence even though arising from universal suffrage, since it can only be used to exploit others by the authorities.[77]

There are for Bakunin three aspects to the development of liberty: first, the full development and enjoyment of all human faculties and powers in each man through upbringing, scientific education and material prosperity, all of which can only be provided by the collective physical and intellectual labor of society as a whole; second, the rebellion of the human individual against all authority, God, the state, etc.; third, rebellion against the tyranny of man, the individual and social authority embodied and legalized by the state.[78]

Convinced that individual and social evils stem far less from individuals than from the organization of things and from social positions, the anarchist revolution will destroy positions and things so as to be able to spare human beings without endangering the revolution. Every human being is the involuntary product of a natural and social environment in which he is

born and reared. The three major causes of all human immorality
are inequality, both political and social, ignorance, and slavery.[79]
The revolution must set out from the first radically and totally to
destroy the state and all state institutions, including revolutionary states, which are just as centralist and despotic as any
others.[80]

Since revolution everywhere must be created by the people,
who must always retain supreme control, Bakunin calls for the
organization of a free federation of agricultural and industrial
associations, organized from the bottom upwards by means of
revolutionary delegation. This form rules out dictatorship and
custodial control. As to the need for a revolutionary agent
Bakunin argues:

> But for the very establishment of the revolutionary alliance and the
> triumph of revolution over reaction, the unity of revolutionary thought
> and action must find an agent in the thick of the populist anarchy which
> will constitute the very life and energy of the revolution. That agent
> must be the secret universal association of international brothers.[81]

The association is not to make or manufacture and direct the
revolution. Rather all it or any such secret society can do is to
assist its birth by sowing ideas corresponding to the instincts of
the masses, a kind of revolutionary general staff made up of the
devoted and sincere friends of the people, without ambition or
vanity, and capable of acting as intermediaries between the
revolutionary idea and the popular instincts.[82] Bakunin felt that
no national revolution could succeed without spreading to all
other nations immediately and that it could not do this unless it
had universal appeal by being socialist in character.[83] This theory
of the necessity for the revolution immediately to spread or
perish is very similar to Trotsky's theory of permanent revolution.

Kropotkin essentially accepted the Bakuninist prescription for
a successful revolution, but with some important modifiers.
Spontaneity there must be, but Kropotkin focuses much more on
the preconditions to the manifestation of spontaneity: long-term
mass education in revolutionary viewpoints more than mere
episodic agitation. Ideas must have become ripe. Moreover,
Kropotkin does not seem to insist on the success of the revolution
hinging on its immediately spreading across the national borders.
Kropotkin sees this as desirable but not essential. Kropotkin

lavishes much time and attention on how to go about building a viable anarchist economy in a given national state and virtually none on the strategy and tactics of spreading the revolution. The implication is that force of successful example will ultimately spread the revolution. Implicit in Kropotkin's life-style was a rejection of the revolutionary activism of Bakunin. While he indulged in anarchist organizational activities, Kropotkin's abstention from revolutionary plots and violent actions did not indicate a lack of commitment or courage but rather an implicit judgment that the masses would have to show signs of revolutionary activity, i.e., a revolutionary situation would clearly have to manifest itself before outright rebellion was advocated by the organization.

The Bakuninist critique of Marx had a profound effect on Kropotkin and the anarchist movement as well. Bakunin differed from Marx in the late 1860s on various questions, some tactical and some matters of principle. Marx was charged with callousness to the aspirations for self-determination of smaller European nationalities looking upon the preservation of the larger political units like Austro-Hungary, as historically more progressive in that they were bigger and hence better economic units. Bakunin championed the causes of the Slavic minorities submerged and subjugated by the Austrians. This is more than a hint of German versus Slavic solidarity involved here. Moreover, Bakunin did not see the unification of Italy and Germany as historically progressive, as many did who welcomed political centralization as the bearer of economic centralization. But the key issue between them in the International in 1869–72 was supposedly that of the impracticality of Bakunin's antiorganizational, proconspiratorial viewpoint.

As Bakunin's writings on the revolutionary organization or brotherhood indicate, he was no enemy of organization. Kropotkin was far more wary of secret organizations, especially hierarchical ones, than Bakunin. As Arthur Lehning indicates, the real issue was whether to accept parliamentary tactics and reliance after the revolution on a dictatorship of the proletariat.[84] Bakunin unequivocally rejected parliamentary tactics and any form of a postrevolutionary state. In 1872 at the Fifth Congress of the International Marx expelled Bakunin by making the conquest of political power obligatory for the whole membership of the International. This marked the historical juncture between the anarchist movement and the Marxists. Bakunin polemicized against this decision by pointing out that a revolutionary state was a contradiction in terms. State implies domination and exploitation. No transitional dictatorships were acceptable. For him the Marxists were worshipers of state power, prophets of political and social discipline, champions of order established from the top downward. Of Marx Bakunin remarks:

I wonder how he manages to overlook the fact that the establishment of a universal dictatorship, collective or individual, a dictatorship which would create the post of a kind of chief engineer of world revolution, ruling and controlling the insurrectionary activity of the masses in all countries ... would in itself suffice to kill revolution and warp and paralyze all popular movements. What man, what group of individuals, no matter how great their genius, would dare to think themselves able to embrace and understand the plethora of interests, attitudes, and activities, so various in every country, province, locality, and profession. . . .[85]

Bakunin accused Marx of pushing for "bourgeois socialism," toward the conclusion of a political pact between the sometimes unwillingly radical bourgeoisie and the intellectual, respectable bourgeois-influenced minority of the urban proletariat, to the exclusion and detriment of the mass of urban and rural proletariat. Even from the standpoint of the urban proletariat who are supposed to reap the chief reward of the seizure of power, the revolution must be a sham. They will wake up slaves and puppets of a new group of ambitious men.[86] Marx promises his state will abolish classes but it will be a complex government, controlling the whole economy. All this will require knowledge:

It will be the reign of the scientific mind, the most aristocratic, despotic, arrogant and contemptuous of regimes. There will be a new class, a new hierarchy of real or bogus learning, and the world will be divided into a dominant, science-based minority and a vast, ignorant majority.[87]

The great mass of people will end up governed by a privileged minority. And if this minority were workers before their apotheosis, they no longer qualify as members of the proletariat once they become rulers or representatives: "Anyone who does not see this does not know anything about human nature."[88]

So Bakunin's secret association will not disappear after the successful revolution. Rather it will remain to watch carefully against the emergence of any authority.[89] This was clearly unacceptable to Kropotkin for at least two reasons: first, it implied the masses were not capable of safeguarding themselves; second, it amounts to an informal version of a permanent "dictatorship of the proletariat," although there are sufficient passages among Bakunin's texts to indicate his abiding disavowal of any form of dictatorship.[90]

What of Bakunin's postrevolutionary stateless society? Labor is to be the basis of all political rights and society will have the power to remove such rights from those who are able to work but refuse to. Idlers might be expelled from the society.[91] All work associations, like individuals, must enjoy absolute liberty. The country must be organized upwards, from the commune to the central unity by way of federation. The basis of any countrywide political organization must be the absolutely autonomous commune, always represented by the majority vote of all the inhabitants. The province must be nothing other than a free federation of communes and the nation nothing other than a federation of autonomous provinces. Ultimately there may be an international federation.[92]

Economic equalty will be a prerequisite for social and political equality. Equality will not mean the leveling down of individual differences or of individual fortunes, insofar as these are due to ability, productive energy, or thrift of the individual. Equality requires the abolition of the right of inheritance. Then, under the influence of an egalitarian social system, individual differences will dwindle in importance although never entirely disappear. All who earn their living by their own work shall have full rights while those who exploit the labor of others or are parasites will have no right to remain in this society.[93] Thus for Bakunin only those who work shall eat, unless they be unable to work. Kropotkin differs with Bakunin on the principle of remuneration for work and refuses to cast parasites or idlers out of society. They too must be supported.

Bakunin sees the distinction between intellectual and manual labor and contempt for the latter as a major cause of inequality: "When the thinker works and the worker thinks, free, intelligent labor will emerge as humanity's highest aspiration. . . ."[94] Here are a theme and an idea which Kropotkin reflected on and amplified at great length. While Bakunin never went beyond tossing the notion out in the form of a principle of the postrevolutionary society, Kropotkin made this idea the inspiration for book-length investigation.

Bakunin goes well beyond Proudhon's limited employment of associated labor. For Bakunin, intelligent free labor will necessarily be associated labor since, while all are free to work alone, or not at all—and suffer the consequences—such association will be generally preferred for the simple reason that it would miraculously increase the productive energies of each associate member, that is increase his earnings and reduce his labor time. As for the peasants, Bakunin, unlike Marx, does not think of them as the backward sector and the backward social class. Presumably they will prefer association in their work but in any case the land, with all its natural resources, belongs to all, but will be held only by those who work it.[95] Bakunin thus sees associations as the overwhelming factor in both industry and agriculture. Proudhon would seem to have expected agriculture to remain a sphere for the individually run family farms.

With the writings of Bakunin and Kropotkin classical anarchism may be said to have fully emerged. The only post-Kropotkin development in world anarchism concerned organizational and tactical rather than intellectual development. I am referring to the advent of a strong anarcho-syndicalist movement in France in the 1880s. From there it spread to Spain. It had only to modify and elaborate Bakuninist and Kropotkinist ideas and principles. Strictly speaking its action program of workers' control, self-management of production in the individual plants, and federations of workers' councils at higher levels, together with the weapons of the general strike, the boycott, sit-ins, and sabotage, were far closer to Bakunin's collectivism than Kropotkin's communism. Its aim of substituting industrial for political action is applied classical anarchism.

CHAPTER 3

Kropotkin's World-View

I The View of Human Nature

IN his justly famous and perhaps most widely read book, *Mutual Aid*, Kropotkin put forward most fully his theory of human nature in an attempt to provide his anarchist theory with a scientific basis. Kropotkin attempts to establish that human morality has its basis in animal and human instinct: more precisely in the instinct of human sociability. Kropotkin's immediate target was to combat the social Darwinism of T. E. Huxley and to rescue Darwinism from the Huxleyites, Spencerians, and Malthusians.

Kropotkin posits that sociability is as much a law of nature as mutual struggle. He takes it as proved that while the struggle for life leads indifferently to both regressive and progressive evolution, the practice of mutual aid is the agency which always leads to progressive development. And, as a factor of evolution, it most probably has a far greater importance since it favors the development of such habits and characters as insure the maintenance and further development of the species together with the greatest amount of welfare and enjoyment of life for the individual, with the least waste of energy.[1] Many species of ants share their food, including that already swallowed and partly digested, with any members of the community which apply for it. Bees are especially cooperative, and to their great advantage. Certain eagles hunt in teams. Pelicans fish together to seal off an area in a circle net. Small birds en masse force larger birds like eagles to drop their food and do not fight over the shares. The longevity of parrots is due to their association and social life. The migration of certain birds is a study in cooperation. Crabs help their fellows who have overturned to right themselves.[2]

Life in societies in the animal world is the norm and reaches its fullest development with the higher vertebrates. Apart from a few exceptions, it is very probable that those birds and mammals which are not now gregarious were living in societies before man multiplied and waged a permanent war against them or destroyed their food sources. As we ascend the scale of evolution, association grows more and more conscious, more reasoned. It moves from the family to the group and finally to associations of groups habitually scattered, but uniting in case of need, e.g., bisons. It takes higher forms guaranteeing more independence to the individual without depriving the individual of the benefits of social life, e.g., individual rodent dwellings laid out in villages. And often it is cultivated and maintained despite the quarrelsomeness of interaction and without being imposed genetically or physiologically, as with ants or bees, in order to insure the benefits of mutual aid, or for the sake of its inherent pleasures. Life in societies allows the weakest birds or mammals to enjoy longevity and protect their progeny and to migrate successfully by means of mutual protection and care. So that while admitting that force, swiftness, protective coloration, running, and endurance make the species or individual the fittest under certain circumstances, Kropotkin holds that under any circumstances sociability yields the greatest advantages in the struggle to survive:

Those species which willingly or unwillingly abandon it are doomed to decay; while those animals which know best how to combine, have the greatest chances of survival and of further evolution, although they may be inferior to others in each of the facilities enumerated by Darwin and Wallace, save the intellectual faculty. The highest vertebrates, and especially mankind, are the best proof of this assertion. As to the intellectual faculty, while every Darwinist will agree with Darwin that it is the most powerful arm in the struggle for life, and the most powerful factor of further evolution, he also will admit that intelligence is eminently social faculty. Language imitation and accumulated experience are so many elements of growing intelligence of which the unsociable animal is deprived. Therefore we find, at the top of each class of animals, the ants, the parrots and the monkeys, all combining the greatest sociability with the highest development of intelligence. The fittest are thus the most sociable animals, and sociability appears as the chief factor of evolution, both directly, by securing the well-being of the species while diminishing the waste of energies, and indirectly, by favoring the growth of intelligence.[3]

Competition is not the rule either in the animal world or in mankind. Its role is limited among animals to exceptional periods. Examples of species survival through mutual aid, through displacing competition, abound: bird migration, hibernation during food short winters, the splitting up of colonies, or resorting to new types of food. All of these are mechanisms to avoid interspecies struggle.[4]

In human societies, individualism is an historic and modern rather than a natural attribute. Primitive man identified his own existence with that of his tribe, and without this communal sentiment there would be no society, no culture. Among the barbarian peoples, private property in land did not exist.[5] The clan or organization provided for stability by assimilating new members so as to preserve the larger group as a defensive and cooperative unit. The law which governed them was customary law. With the growth of cities in the Middle Ages, self-administration was the norm. The medieval city was more than simply a political organization; it was a close union for mutual aid and support.[6]

Despite the eventual subjugation and impoverishment of the free cities and free peasants by the forces of national consolidation and centralization through wars, taxes, and industrialization, there survives a vital underlay of communal customs and habits of mutual aid coupled with important vestiges of communal possession of the sort. And this rural, communal vitality manifests itself when conditions allow. Kropotkin observes:

> In short, neither the crushing powers of the centralized State nor the teachings of mutual hatred and pitiless struggle which comes adorned with the attributes of science, from obliging philosophers and sociologists, could weed out the feeling of human solidarity, deeply lodged in man's understanding and heart, because it has been nurtured by all over preceding evolution.[7]

Clearly, for Kropotkin, mankind's achievements past and future are due to the practice of mutual aid, and this is an irrepressible phenomenon which will survive counterideologies and their institutional progeny. Kropotkin's theoretical search for what his disciple and biographer N. Lebedev called "the physics of human conduct" did not end with *Mutual Aid*. His last theoretical effort on this subject began in 1918, after his return to Russia. Only one of two projected volumes was to emerge in manuscript form, and it is not quite complete. It represents an attempt to account for the origin of man's moral conceptions and to examine the goals or aims of moral conduct.

Whereas Kropotkin's *Mutual Aid* had clearly denied any connection between morality, as he defined it, and religion or metaphysics, the goal of *Ethics* was to establish a moral imperative on a purely naturalistic, scientific basis. A scientific ethics was for Kropotkin what the laws of dialectical and historical materialism were for Marx and the Marxists: a scientific basis for his revolutionary optimism and projections of a workable postrevolutionary society based on equality, fraternity, justice, and material well-being. In the later work Kropotkin builds upon the biological research of *Mutual Aid* to delve into the development of mankind's history, philosophy, and economics in order to account for the genesis, development, and ascendancy of ethical principles held or shared by various societies.

The history of ideas and institutions is portrayed as a battleground in which science struggles to roll back ignorance and metaphysical ideologies. Establishing the biological imperative of an ethical code will prove the key to unlocking ideological barriers against the ultimate rationalization of society.

Here Kropotkin lays claim to Darwin as intellectual ally and ascendant. He presents Darwin as having traced the foundation of all moral feelings to those instincts which lead the animal to take pleasure in society:

Being thus necessary for the preservation, the welfare, and the progressive development of every species, the mutual aid instinct has become what Darwin described as "a permanent instinct," which is always at work in all social animals, and especially in man. Having its origins at the very beginning of the evolution of the animal world, it's certainly an instinct as deeply seated in animals, low and high, as the instinct of material love; .... Darwin was therefore quite right in considering that the instinct of "mutual sympathy" is more permanently at work in the social animals than even the purely egotistic instinct or direct self-preservation. He saw in it, as is known, the rudiments of the moral conscience, which consideration is, unfortunately, too often forgotten by the Darwinists.[8]

Kropotkin sees in this instinct the origins of those benevolent feelings which lead to the partial identification of the individual with the group. And upon this foundation arises a higher sense of justice, as well as a spirit of self-sacrifice. The more highly evolved the species, the more highly developed is the sense of identification of individual with group interests. This, for Kropotkin, indicates the natural origins of ethics. Moral codes are not a branch of metaphysics but are a creation of men who reflect on what they see and inherit from nature. And these are the reflections not of exceptional individuals but of ordinary men.[9]

Kropotkin holds that historical investigations make it possible to conceive of man's history as the evolution of an ethical factor. The idea of man as an isolated being is a product of later civilization, unknown to primitive men. There never was any state of nature in which individuals lived in splendid isolation and self-sufficiency and from which they begrudgingly emerged to form mutual-protection associations called states. There is and has been no social contract to check the inherent depravity of the species; social life, the "we," not the "I," is the norm.

Deriving the general rule of mutual aid from observing the species solidarity of carnivorous beasts and from his own inadequacy to cope with dangers and complex tasks, primitive man acquired the habit of limiting his will by the will of others. Here, in the absorption of the "I" by the clan or tribe, lies the root of all ethical thought. The gradual transition from this simple abstract of cooperation with similar creatures to the concept of mutual relations regulated by a moral code becomes necessary for the sake of pursuing social life itself, declares Kropotkin:

> In the life of human societies a very long period of time must, of necessity, elapse before the majority of the members learn to subordinate their first spontaneous impulses to the considerations of more or less remote consequences. The habit of subordinating one's unconscious tendencies to social considerations on the basis of personal experience, develops first in separate individuals, and then the great multitude of such individual inductions combines into tribal morality, supported by tradition and transmitted from generation to generation.[10]

Kropotkin's historicism is clear. The problem of moral philosophy—why men are capable of thinking and feeling in terms of others—is inseparable from the skein of natural and social history. Conscience emerges from the consciousness of equity which physiologically develops in man as in all social animals; it becomes as natural as the need for nourishment. Man, that supreme social animal, can see himself in the sufferings of others, and through this primary identification sympathy evolves into the concept of equity and justice.

The linear development of ethical standards and productive potential have led, according to Kropotkin, to a privileged historical moment in history:

> For the first time in the history of civilization, mankind has reached a point where the means of satisfying its needs are in excess of the needs themselves to impose, therefore, as has hitherto been done, the curse of misery and degradation upon vast divisions of mankind, in order to secure well-being and further mental development for the few, is needed no more: well-being can be secured for all, without placing on anyone the burden of oppressive, degrading toil, and humanity can at last rebuild its entire social life on the bases of justice.[11]

Christian ethics, intent on grooming the private soul, and economic individualism, the rapacious ideology of European capitalism, can only shackle historical progress.

Since Kropotkin's "ethics" are biologically mandated, they must be distinguished from the relativist "class ethics" of Marx. Yet Kropotkin stops short of predicting victory for "justice" over the competing instincts of self-preservation and egoism through the inevitable operation of natural law. More than scientific analysis, it is perhaps his own moral fervor which so imbued Kropotkin with his vision of morality as the historical destiny of man.

II   Revolutionary Tactics and Goals

The chief sources of Kropotkin's views on revolutionary tactics and strategy, on the role of the revolutionary party, and on the immediate postrevolutionary situation are to be found in his first book, *Paroles d'un Revolte* (1886), and in his two-volume *The Great French Revolution* (1909).

Kropotkin believed that the times were revolutionary because of the people's having awakened to the moral, intellectual, and economic failure of the ruling class. Class consciousness emerges chiefly through direct experience of poverty and unemployment rather than, as with Marx, through critical analysis by the individual which emerges as class consciousness. In other words, for Kropotkin, "class consciousness" is spontaneous; for Marx, analytical. Kropotkin, like Marx, sees recurrent economic crises as the symptom of capitalism's failure. Capital invests in areas of little social value, especially war expenditures. Mature capitalism involves increasing foreign investments and more and more speculation. It gradually dawns on the population that capitalism is unable to sustain a smooth and equitable system of production and exchange.[12] Imperialism and interimperialist rivalries ultimately accelerate the collapse of nation states as imperialist wars turn into civil wars between the classes.[13] All this is the result of the lust for profit scorning all social laws.[14] Clearly Kropotkin is not here referring to Marx's laws of historical materialism, which have nothing to do with moral categories whose empirical subjects are concrete individuals, and operate automatically, scientifically, impersonally. Moreover, Kropotkin's vision of capitalism's end is not based on any theoretically insoluble economic contradictions inherent in the system. Rather the economic crises that do ultimately lead to revolution are themselves rooted in moral failure: "greed," "lust," "wars." Still, the vision of a "finale" for capitalism born of a great industrial crisis superficially coincides with that of Marx.[15]

Kropotkin holds that the next revolution will not be limited to a mere change in the personnel or the power holders. Rather it will be international in scope, encompassing all of Europe. And the people will not want for constituted authorities to grant them rights. Rather they will "take" their rights. There will be no need for legitimacy to be bestowed from on high. This revolution will come from below.[16] Real political rights are never given. They must be seized.[17]

Kropotkin admits that the anarchist-communists are a small minority. Numbers, he holds, are not important. What is important is that anarchist ideas conform to realities. History is evolving progressively toward common production and consumption and the coincidence of the moral, political, and economic spheres. Kropotkin believes that aspirations for equality, communist distribution, etc., "are born in the very entrails of the people."[18] Thus concepts, for Kropotkin, are a product of historical rather than theoretical genesis, as with Marx.

Kropotkin saw the many millions of rural poor as a major

source of revolutionary material. He saw the large-scale mechanization of agricultural power as having dramatically changed the European peasantry over the last thirty years. The tax burden on the peasants and their displacement to the cities and the consequent further concentration of land in the hands of fewer and fewer rentiers given to unproductive consumption was giving rise to revolutionary combustibles.[19] Millions of peasant proprietors all over Europe, especially in France, were being driven toward the subsistence level. The middle peasant, defined as one holding between ten and fifty hectares, was becoming politically conscious. These peasants do not trust armies, and peasants with interests to protect constitute, says Kropotkin, the most formidable armies.[20] Thus Kropotkin, unlike Marx, gives pride of place in the revolutionary future to the peasantry.

Kropotkin warns against pseudosocialist revolutionaries, insisting on the unity of theory and practice. Real socialists must insist on the abolition of wage labor and private property in the means of production and mineral wealth. They must practice socialism in their private lives. He warns against bourgeois impostors who enter the revolutionary movement only to deflect and dilute it from within. He also warns against so-called socialists who would postpone the revolution to some distant future, say 200 years ahead. They are preoccupied with realizable reforms. They are either incrementalists or opportunists.[21] Kropotkin insists on a revolutionary vision, on postrevolutionary goals. He insists that no political action is independent of a point of view.[22] But all true socialists can agree on the necessity of expropriating capital. Around this primary principle a popular front can be formed.[23]

Kropotkin generated a theoretical perspective on the future revolution by studying in particular the great French Revolution and the Paris Commune of 1871. In both there was a failure of boldness of thought and example to induce the masses to execute what they had dared to think. Moreover, past revolutionaries "dared not destroy enough to open wide the gates, and of that new life their conceptions were so vague and consequently so timid, so narrow, that they dared not, even in their dreams, touch the fetishes which they had adored in their past slavery."[24] Science has revealed as frauds the divine origins of human institutions and the so-called laws of providence which have served to explain and perpetuate slavery. Man has been able to see that he makes his institutions and that he alone can remake them. Science has also accelerated the revolutionary impetus by undermining the idea of stability which had hitherto attached to everything which man saw in nature. Now science has demonstrated that everything is incessantly modified: systems, wages, planets, climates, animals, plants, and *homo sapiens.* Why would human institutions perpetuate themselves? And so we come to see revolution is an essential part of evolution, that no evolution is accomplished in nature without revolutions. Life is a continual development and the plant, animal, individual, or society which sticks fast will perish.[25]

As to means, the massacre of the bourgeoisie cannot secure the triumph of the revolution. The roots of the bourgeois mentality must be extirpated, not the symbols, symptoms, or products of it. Moreover, the organized and legalized terror necessary to do this can only forge chains for the people. Terror kills individual initiative, which is the soul of revolution. It perpetuates the idea of obedience to a strong government. People must understand that the true work of a popular revolution is to destroy the state, which is necessarily hierarchical, and to sweep away elected governments which have substituted themselves for the free consent of all.[26] In the revolutions of the past the people rebelled but left the work of revolutionary reorganization to the bourgeoisie.[27]

Kropotkin defines a revolution as:

... the fall, the crumbling away in a brief period, of all that up to that time composed the essence of social, religious, political and economic life in a nation. It means the subversion of acquired ideas and of accepted notions concerning each of the complex institutions and relations of the human herd.[28]

For a revolution to occur:

The revolutionary action coming from the people must coincide with a movement of revolutionary thought coming from the educated classes. There must be a union of the two.[29]

The soul of the French revolution for Kropotkin was the peasant insurrection:

Upon it the struggle of the middle classes for their political rights was developed. Without it the revolution would never have been so thorough as it was in France.[30]

Kropotkin sees the French revolution as above all a movement by the peasants to regain possession of the land and to free it from feudal obligation. While admitting that this involved a powerful individualist element, there was also, he asserts, a communist element: the right of the whole nation to the land.[31]

The first attempts at constituting communes were made by popular initiative in Paris. To this experiment in direct self-government, Kropotkin attributes great importance:

> We thus see that the principles of anarchism, expressed some years later in England by W. Godwin, already dated from 1789, and that they had their origins not in theoretical speculations, but in the deeds of the Great French Revolution.[32]

The Lyon workers demanded that wages should be regulated by the commune and be such as to guarantee subsistence. It was also proposed that the communes take over the industrial enterprises abandoned by the counterrevolutionaries and operate them for themselves. Says Kropotkin:

> On the whole, it was the problem of the means of subsistence that was the preoccupation of the communists of 1793, and led them to compel the convention to pass the law of maximum, and also to formulate the great principle of the socialization of the exchange of produce—the municipalisation of trade.
>
> We then see, budding during the Revolution, the idea that commerce is a social function; that it must be socialised, as well as the land and the industries—an idea which was to be elaborated later on by Fourier, Robert Owen, Proudhon, and the communists of the forties.[33]

But by the end of 1793 the revolution was arrested in its development. A revolution that stops halfway is sure to be defeated. Its energies were now spent in internal struggles and in attempts to exterminate its enemies and divide the loot. All those who had made fortunes by the Revolution were now in a hurry to return to a state of "order."[34] Still, France emerged as the richest country of Europe because of the revolution. Why? Because of the redistribution of wealth, primarily in land, that resulted.[35]

As to the revolutionary party, Kropotkin rejects the introduction of any hierarchy of ranks as a violation of the equality of all members. Nor does he condone the use of deception or coercion as revolutionary tactics. And the business of a revolutionary party is not to call for insurrection but rather to pave the way for the success of the imminent insurrection. There can be no revolution unless the need for it is felt by the people.[36] In a letter of March 5, 1902, to Max Nettlau, Kropotkin emphasizes the folly of believing that a few strong revolutionaries could incite a revolution. Commenting on the Russian revolution of 1905, Kropotkin gives all the credit for taking the lead to the workers, not to any of the revolutionary parties.[37]

The revolution develops spontaneously without being orchestrated by a Leninist party. And the economic change which will emerge from its victory is so profound, declares Kropotkin, it is impossible to elaborate in advance the different social forms which will spring up in its wake. This elaboration can only be improvised by the collective work of the masses.[38] Thus there can be for Kropotkin no "dictatorship of the proletariat" for even a short transitional period and certainly no revolutionary government, for this is a contradiction in terms.

In the wake of the revolution there must be expropriation extending to all means of production that permit the appropriation of the product of another's labor. The real science of economics will then be installed as the basis for the new society. Scientific economics is the study of the needs of humanity and of the economic means to satisfy these.[39] Thus, "bread for all" is the slogan of the triumphant revolution. The first step to be taken after its success is to do everything necessary to assure shelter, food, and clothes for all. Kropotkin is supremely confident that the people's powers of self-organization will quickly solve this problem: "Give the people a free hand, and in ten days the food service will be conducted with admirable regularity."[40]

In any case, says Kropotkin, what would ensue would hardly be worse than the previous conditions, and a system which springs up spontaneously under the stress of immediate need is infinitely preferable to anything invented by "hidebound theorists sitting on any number of committees."[41] All that the community possesses in abundance will be distributed freely. But there will be equal sharing of those commodities which are scarce. He has absolute faith in the people's fairness.[42]

If the revolution were to break out simultaneously all over Europe, expropriation and reorganization would be simplified, but Kropotkin thinks this unlikely.

The food supply will at first be aggravated by the severing of the parasitic ties of the imperalist mother countries from their raw material and food-supplying colonies. The end result, however, will benefit both colony and mother country, for it will force the European country to strive for self-sufficiency in agriculture through intensified production and more rational combinations of industry and agriculture.[43] Kropotkin advocates total expropriation of all housing and the right of each family to a decent dwelling.[44] He cites the traditional role of the Russian village commune in redistributing fields as evidence of the people's ability to redistribute housing.[45] As for equitable food distribution, Kropotkin can point to the experience of the Paris commune.

What about the role of art in the ideal society? For Kropotkin, art is at the service of humanity and great art should be comprehensible to the masses.[46] Since there will be no central government, there can be no control over aesthetics or publication. Aesthetic standards must emerge individually and must be intimately associated with the internalized scientific ethics that form the *modus operandi* of the anarchist society.

III   *Anarchist-Communism: The Transcendence of Capitalism*

According to Kropotkin the anarchist does not resort to metaphysical conceptions such as "natural rights" or "the duties of the state." Rather the anarchist studies societies past and present in order to find out the best way to combine the needs of the individual with cooperation for the welfare of the species. He searches for the critical tendencies of social evolution and for the causes frustrating or retarding their progress. Kropotkin cites the two most prominent, often unconscious historical tendencies: first, the integration of labor for the production of all wealth in common so as to render it impossible to decide which part is attributable to one particular individual; second, the development of the fullest freedom of the individual to pursue all beneficial goals for both himself and society. The ideal of the anarchist is thus to usher in the next stage of social evolution rather than to fulfill a messianic role.[47]

Kropotkin notes what he calls the present unparalleled accumulation of wealth but sees it increasingly concentrated in the hands of the capitalist class. At the same time the overwhelming majority suffer increased misery and insecurity. With the spread of knowledge the demand for equality on the part of the downtrodden masses will grow.

Kropotkin sees more and more questioning of the state's role as the sponsor of progress. He feels that a further advance in social life does not lie in the direction of further concentration of power and regulatory functions in the state but rather in the direction of decentralization, both territorial and functional. The initiative must pass to freely constituted groups for all those functions now considered governmental. Representative government is simply the rule of the dominant class or classes under capitalism. It must be transcended by the "no-government" system.[48] The practicality of this transcendence is substantiated, says Kropotkin, by analogy to the natural world:

By bringing to light the plasticity of organization, the philosophy of evolution has shown the admirable adaptability of organisms to their conditions of life, and the ensuing development of such facilities as render more complete both the adaptations of the aggregates to their surroundings and those of each of the constituent parts of the aggregate to the needs of free cooperation. It has familiarized us with the circumstance that throughout organic nature the capacities for life in common grow in proportion as the integration of organisms into compound aggregates becomes more and more complete; and it has enforced thus the opinion already expressed by social moralists as to the perfectibility of human nature.[49]

Kropotkin sees social wealth and knowledge as having been created by the common efforts of mankind and thus as belonging to all equally. What we have today is in good measure the result of the labor and genesis of past generations. Everything belongs to all! Who can say what share of the general wealth is due to each individual, he asks:

And provided each man and woman contributes his and her share of labour for the production of necessary objects, they have a right to share in all that is produced by everybody.[50]

An equitable organization of society can only arise when all wage systems are abandoned and when all who contribute to the common well-being to the fullest extent of their capabilities enjoy to the fullest the satisfaction of their needs. Kropotkin sees evidence of the growth of the communist tendency despite the

entrenched egoist ethics of capitalism. And as humanity is
relieved from its hard struggle for life, that is, as the productive
powers grow stronger and more capable of providing everyone
with the necessities, and as the present leisure class becomes
productive, the communist principle of distribution will extend.
Ultimately anarchist-communism, the synthesis of the two chief
aims pursued by humanity from the dawn of history—economic
and political freedom—will emerge.

This will not be barracks-room or monastic communism,
declares Kropotkin:

> We foresee millions and millions of groups freely constituting
> themselves for the satisfaction of all the varied needs of human beings
> ... and after having performed their share of productive labour will
> meet together, either for the purpose of consumption or to produce
> objects of art or luxury, or to advance science. ...[51]

Despite the obvious economies obtainable through communal
preparation of foods and communal dining, Kropotkin
emphasized:

> ...no one has a right to force the housewife to take her potatoes from
> the communal kitchen ready cooked if she prefers to cook them herself
> in her own pot on her own fire; and, above all, we should wish each one
> to be free to take his meals with his family, or with his friends, or even
> in a restaurant, if it seemed good to him.[52]

Anarchist-communism will combine three elements: first,
emancipation of the producer from the yoke of capital. This
means production in common followed by free consumption of
all the products of common labor. Second, emancipation from
the governmental yoke, that is, free development of individuals
in groups and federations, free organization ascending from the
simple to the complex, according to mutual needs and tendencies. Third, emancipation from religious morality; that means
free morality without compulsion of authority, spontaneously
developing from social life and becoming habitual. So long as
communism presented itself in an authoritarian form which
implied government it had little appeal. But anarchist-communism maintains individual liberty and extends it most importantly
to the economic realm. One must not accept a party as a
surrogate god. Rather than attempting to reconsruct society

from the top down, society should be allowed to develop unfettered, from the simple to the composite, by the free union of groups. Anarchy must mean no rulers, no ruled, no trust in representatives.[53]

IV *The Role of the State*

For Kropotkin the state in European history is of recent origin, barely going back to the sixteenth century. All animals live in societies. Therefore man did not in any sense create society. Rather, society existed before man—and human society before the state. The Middle Ages saw the zenith of free cities. These became centers of well-being for all their inhabitants such as we have not seen since. They were free of the poverty, insecurity and physical exploitation characteristic of present capitalism. The breadth of freedom and the depth of skill and pride in their artisan skills and the brotherhood fostered by the guilds created a sociability more than just commercial. The level of the arts and industries attained a perfection which modern times have only been able to surpass in speed and scale of production but rarely in quality or the intrinsic beauty of the product. The compass, clock, printing, gunpowder, maritime discoveries, laws of gravitation, rudiments of chemistry, Bacon's scientific method—all originated in the free cities. In the sixteenth century the modern barbarians destroyed this wonderful medieval matrix. They destroyed all the liberties and all ties between men, declaring that the state and the church alone would henceforth mediate between their subjects.[54]

The statist socialists would use the state under their auspices to revive the spirit of federation, individualism, and self-initiative which it crushed. Throughout history two opposing traditions or tendencies have confronted each other: the Roman, imperial, or authoritarian and the popular, federalist, or libertarian. And on the eve of a new social revolution, states Kropotkin, they still do:

Either the state forever crushing individual and local life, taking over in all fields of human authority, bringing with it wars and its domestic struggles for power, its palace revolutions which only replace one tyrant by another ... or the destruction of the state, and new life starting again in thousands of centers on the principle of the lively initiative of the individual and groups and that of free agreement.[55]

Anarchism is the representative of the creative, constructive power of the people who aim at freeing themselves from the power-seeking minority. Anarchism aims at creating a society in which relationships are regulated not by authorities, whether the latter are self-proclaimed or elected, but rather by mutual agreements between members, and by social customs and habits not petrified and enslaved by law, superstition, or authorities, but continually developed and readjusted in accordance with the ever-growing requirements of a free life. This process abolishes government of man by man and replicates the continuous evolution of nature. This situation means free play for the individual without fear of punishment.[56]

The state and capitalism are inseparable concepts. Historically, they developed side by side, mutually supporting and reinforcing each other, and are bound together not by a mere coincidence of contemporaneous development but by the bond of cause and effect, effect and cause. The state is a society for the mutual assurance of the landlord, the warrior, the judge, and the priest, constituted in order to enable them to assert their authority over the people and to exploit the poor. It is therefore absurd to hope to abolish capitalism and yet maintain the state. A new form of economic organization necessarily requires a new form of political structure, and these two changes must go on together. Socialism must find its own form of political organization. And this organization must involve the abolition of the state and the broadest possible development of the principle of free agreement and free association.[57]

All past progress, intellectual and moral, is due to the practice of mutual aid, to the customs that recognized the equality of men and united them in protection and consumption. Communist organization cannot be constructed by legislatures. Rather it must be the work of all, a natural growth, a product of the constructive genius of the great mass. Communism cannot be imposed from above. It must be free.[58]

V   *Anarchist Morality Replaces Law and Authority*

Social feelings of solidarity which alone made society possible are anterior to law and religion. They are found among all social animals. They are in fact ultimately instinctual, says Kropotkin:

The hospitality of primitive peoples, respect for human life, the sense of reciprocal obligation, compassion for the weak, extending even to the sacrifice of self for others which is first learned for the sake of children and friends, and later for that of members of the same community—all these qualities are developed in man anterior to all law, independently of all religion, as in the case of the social animals. Such feelings and practices are the inevitable results of social life.[59]

Unfortunately, habits and customs are evolved in human association such as the desire to dominate and to accumulate the fruits of another's labor. Law is introduced to sanctify the fruits of aggression in the hands of the aggressor class. Most laws exist to protect the wealth acquired through the exploitation of man by man, to rob the producer of a part of what he has created. To the extent that laws exist to protect individuals they are ineffectual. Crimes committed by the deranged are relatively insignificant and not preventable by law. If crimes against persons other than those motivated by economic deprivation lessen, it is due to a growth in humanitarian social habits. Hence Kropotkin urges:

No more laws! No more judges! Liberty, equality and practical human sympathy are the only effectual barriers we can oppose to the anti-social instincts of certain among us.[60]

Underlying what is considered conventional morality or good conduct is conduct useful for the preservation of mankind. The idea of good and evil is a natural need of animal species. The moral sense is as natural a faculty as the sense of smell. Equality is equity. We do not wish to be ruled, so we must must not rule others.[61] Yet equality is not enough. If society practiced merely the equity of the trader, with individuals taking care not to give to others anything more than they received from them, social life would die. That which mankind most admires and needs in truly moral people is their exuberance, their generosity, their expense of self without asking the equivalent in return. The man overflowing with intellectuality naturally seeks to diffuse his ideas. There is no pleasure in thinking unless the thought is communicated.[62]

But how would society function without law and authority, with only voluntary agreements unenforceable in court? And how would people be compensated for their labor? What incentives would exist for all to work if necessities were provided regardless of labor? The point of departure for Kropotkin's answer is that in the civilized nations work is a habit, a norm, and idleness is the exception, an artificial condition. Overwork is repulsive to human nature, not work. Work is a physiological necessity; that is, one must expend one's accumulated bodily energy. In reality the indolent are a product of capitalist society. The lazy and the criminal elements are products of a system which victimizes them.

Kropotkin poses the paradox: in our rich, civilized societies why are there so many poor? Why do even employed workers face the fear of future unemployment in the midst of the immense riches of techniques and knowledge we now possess? Kropotkin holds that the present level of development of the productive forces is adequate to assure all the necessities and more in return for a few hours of daily labor. He finds the root cause of widespread poverty in a system which allows natural resources, technology, food, shelter, education, knowledge, and land to be seized by the few. They reduce the masses to the point at which they lack the means of subsistence and have to work for the monopolist-employers for a mere fraction of the value they create with their labor. Production is based on producing whatever returns the greatest profit to the monopolists, not on providing for social needs.

Kropotkin argues that each of the atoms comprising what we call the wealth of nations owes its value to the fact that it is a part of the greater whole. What, he asks, could be the value of a London dockyard or a Paris warehouse if they were not situated in these great centers of international commerce? Millions of people labored to create this civilization and other millions all over the world continue to do so to maintain it. Even the common fund of man's ideas is composed of social products despite their individual genesis, states Kropotkin:

> There is not even a thought, or an invention, which is not common property, born of the past and the present ... every new invention is a synthesis, the resultant of innumerable inventions which have preceded it in the vast field of mechanics and industry.[63]

By what right then can anyone appropriate the last morsel of this immense whole and say it is his alone? The means of production being the collective work of humanity should be the collective property of the race. Individual appropriation is neither just nor serviceable. All things are for all men since all have need of them and all have in some measure contributed to their production and maintenance, and since it is not possible to evaluate every individual's part in the production of the world's wealth. If an individual does his fair share of work, he or she is entitled to a fair share of all that is produced. Everyone is entitled to well-being.[64]

If the leisure class were forced to perform useful work, wealth would further expand. And we know that despite Malthus, the oracle of middle-class economics, the productive powers of the human race increase at a much more rapid rate than the rate of human reproduction. Kropotkin cites the statistic that, from 1842 to 1890, the English population increased by 62 percent and its production by 130 percent, at the least. And this in spite of a tremendous increase in the ranks of the idlers and middlemen. Moreover, the owners of capital constantly reduce output by restraining production and putting millions out of work. Another indirect limitation on production is the decision by employers to expend much human labor on luxury goods or useless objects, especially armaments for war.[65] Patents are bought up in order to suppress progress.[66] And war is nothing but organized national looting for the benefit of the capitalists. Kropotkin concludes: it involves imperialism, colonialism, the search for new markets, raw materials, and profits:

> When we fight now-a-days it is to insure The Factory of Kings a bonus of thirty percent, to strengthen the "Barons" of finance in their hold on the money market, and to keep up the rate of interest for shareholders. . . . If we were only consistent, we should replace the lion on our standard with a golden calf, their other emblems of money bags, and the names of our regiments, borrowed formerly from royalty, by the titles of the kings of industry and finance—"Third Rothschild," "Tenth Baring," etc. We should at least know whom we were killing for.[67]

Clearly Kropotkin focuses on the productive potential of redistribution in postrevolutionary society. Writing in *The Conquest of Bread*, he hazards that by working fifty half-days in a well-organized society the population would be dressed better than the present lower middle class. He calculates that only sixty half-days work of five hours could provide food, only forty for housing, and 150 days would be left for providing other necessities.[68]

In the anarchist future, the scope and nuance of needs will grow and vary as the conquest of bread is won and the free and full development of the individual becomes an end in itself.[69]

And the nature of work will change. The work place must accommodate the individual; factory, forge, and mine can be made as healthy an environment as the finest laboratories. In this vision Kropotkin makes it clear he does not favor a total merger of work and leisure, home and job; he wants no socialization of privacy. Isolation, alternating with time spent in society, is the normal desire of human nature.[70]

But work must become more than drudgery reinforced by the classical economists' negative incentive: the threat of hunger. For Kropotkin the satisfaction of physical, artistic, and moral needs has always been the most powerful stimulant to work. He concludes:

Suppress the cause of idleness, and you may take it for granted that only a few individuals will really hate work, and that there will be no need to manufacture a code of laws on their account.[71]

Kropotkin's approach to remuneration or the wage system is thoroughly communist. He breaks with those collectivists who are willing to recognize distinctions between skilled and unskilled labor. To do so perpetuates class distinctions. Kropotkin looks upon such differences as socially determined and hence as eradicable by equal access to knowledge and training. The privileges of education must be effaced. Services rendered to society must not continue to be valued in money, nor can reward be geared to output or time worked. He does not speak of a system of group or collective payments but rather dismisses any payment system. There can be no exact measure of value or of use value in terms of production. Need must be given priority in distribution; first of all rights is the right to life and then the right to well-being.[72]

VI   *Kropotkin as Reformer: Toward the Establishment of a More Just Society*

Kropotkin's vision of an anarchist-communist society did not dampen his enthusiasm in advocating certain reforms as immediately adaptable. In a major collection of essays entitled *Fields, Factories and Workshops*, he discussed the many advantages of combining industrial and agricultural work with a thorough integration of manual and mental work. This combination involved in the broadest sense fundamental decentralization of economic life in industrial societies and a new approach to education. Kropotkin also became a major proponent of penal reforms and advocated a fundamental reconsideration of the *raison d'être* of orthodox penal theory, based in good measure on his own experiences recounted in a book entitled *In Russian and French Prisons*.

Kropotkin begins his argument for decentralizing industries by bemoaning the conventional wisdom of orthodox economists to the effect that prosperity lies in the further enhancement of the division of labor—a process which has, says Kropotkin, already destroyed the skilled artisan who found aesthetic enjoyment in the work of his hands and which has replaced him with the human slave of an iron slave who makes the eighteenth part of a pin. Having succeeded in perfecting the dehumanized division of labor on an individualized basis within industries, these economists now proclaim their desire to universalize specialization on a regional and national scale. Kropotkin preaches that variety in work is a need both of individuals and societies. With the global spread of knowledge and technology, each nation will acquire a broader scope for its energies. Knowledge ignores artificial political boundaries. Kropotkin holds that the present tendency of humanity is to maximize in the nation and in each region the greatest possible variety of industries side by side with agriculture. Kropotkin boldly proclaims that the state toward which society is already marching is one of integrated labor:

A society where each individual is a producer of both manual and intellectual work; where each able-bodied human being is a worker, and where each worker works both in the field and the industrial workshops; where each aggregation of individuals large enough to dispose of a certain variety of natural resources—it may be a nation or rather a region—produces and itself consumes most of its own agricultural and manufactured produce.[73]

The global trend toward decentralization of industry and integration of industry and agriculture meant that each nation would become a manufacturing nation, with even the most backward ultimately becoming capable of producing everything it might need.[74]

Turning to agriculture, that stronghold of Malthusian theory, Kropotkin denies that natural resources must inevitably fail to supply the means to existence for an increasing population. Kropotkin delves into the virtually unlimited prospects for agricultural intensification and discusses future overpopulation fears as groundless:

> Our means of obtaining from the soil whatever we want, under any climate and upon any soil, have lately been improved at such a rate that we cannot foresee yet what is the limit of productivity of a few acres of land.[75]

The rational method of conducting agriculture would avoid the extremes of small, isolated family farms and gigantic, impersonal farms worked by "labor battalions." The latter conserve on human labor but tend to exhaust the soil while the former waste labor while getting good quality products. In agriculture, as in everything else, Kropotkin holds associated labor to be the only reasonable solution.[76]

As to the association of industry and agriculture, Kropotkin concedes that the trend is clearly toward the absorption of small industries by larger ones. Yet there is also a continuous creation of new industries, usually constituted at first on a small scale. Each new factory calls into existence a number of small workshops, partly to supply its own needs and partly to process its products. This situation stimulates the birth of new petty trades by creating new needs.[77] Thus to some extent, small trades and small industries are viable.

Kropotkin's optimism about the viability of small industries was based on new developments in transportation and the advent of small motors for supplying power. And he pointed out that the advantage of large factories over small ones was often not a technical one but rather lay in combining the selling of these products and the buying of the necessary raw materials to effect competitive advantages at both ends. Wherever this difficulty can be overcome, either by means of association or by finding a market, the associated small producers could adapt tech-nologically by inventing new machine tools or utilizing new motors and cutting their production costs. Small industries normally fail not because they are less economical but rather because the large capitalist emancipates himself from the wholesale and retail dealers in raw materials and need not deal with the ultimate buyers. He can sell inferior goods because of large quantity sales. With the increasing significance of distant markets, this works against the survival of small trade producers.[78] Hence Kropotkin's desire for regions to develop a mixed agro-industrial base so as to work toward regional or local autarky and undercut the larger firm's marketing advantage.

If peasants are not driven off the land, they will turn to various trades in addition to farming. In fact the petty trades can thrive in combination with agriculture. Kropotkin is not suggesting a return to handwork if machines can save on human labor. He is not a modern Luddite calling for the destruction of machinery. Rather he points out that under a more rational social organization the factory could be a boon to the village. Kropotkin also admits that to some degree the huge centralized industries gathering thousands of workers in one site are necessary. But many are nothing else but agglomerations under a common management and several distinct industries, while others are merely concentrations of duplicative activities, such as the gigantic spinning and weaving establishments. From a technical point of view, these latter operations show little if any advantage. As to the production of goods which derive their value chiefly from the skilled labor expended on their production, they can be best fabricated in smaller factories which employ a few hundred. And as new branches of industry must make a start on a smaller scale, they can prosper in smaller towns.[79] Often industries are artifically concentrated in cities. Yet agriculture, being essentially seasonal, needs urban labor during harvests, and has excessive unemployed or underemployed labor in winter. If factories were scattered in the country, an optimal combination of field and factory work might come about. It could also bring about a combination of manual and mental labor.[80]

The division of labor has sharply separated mental and physical work. The worker sentenced to specialization has lost intellectual interest in his labor; he has lost his inventiveness. Formerly manual workers invented or perfected the motors and machinery which revolutionized industry over the last 100 years. This creativity has been smothered by assembly-line monotony.[81]

Yet it is in the interest of both science and industry that everyone receive an education which allows him to combine a thorough knowledge of science with a handicraft skill. While specialized knowledge is necessary, general education in both science and the crafts is needed.[82] The railway engine, the phonograph, the weaving machine, the lace machine, the macadamized road, and black and white and color photography were invented by men who were artisans or craftsmen:

> Those men—the Watts and the Stephensons—knew something which the savants do not know—they knew the use of their hands; their surroundings stimulated their inventive powers; they knew machines. . . .[83]

Overwhelmingly the mechanical invention came before the discovery of the scientific law—the telegraph before a theory of electricity, the steam engine before the dynamic theory of heat. The term "applied science" is quite misleading because more often inventions, far from being applications of science, on the contrary create new branches of science.[84] While all do not have the temperament for scientific work, all would be more useful in their work if they possessed a serious scientific knowledge. And those with scientific knowledge would also benefit if they spent a part of their lives in the workshops or farm, if they were in contact with men in their daily work and had the satisfaction of knowing that they personally discharged their duties as unprivileged producers of wealth.[85]

Kropotkin exudes optimism about the ability of society to solve the production problem:

> Modern knowledge tells us that in order to be rich men need not take the bread from the mouths of others. Machinery, science and cooperative organization will reduce the time necessary for producing wealth to any desired amount, so as to leave everyone as much leisure as he or she may ask for. They surely cannot guarantee happiness, because happiness depends as much, or even more, upon the individual himself as upon his surroundings. But they guarantee, at least, the happiness that can be found in the full and varied exercise of the different capacities of the human being, in work that need not be overwork, and in the consciousness that one is not endeavoring to base his own happiness upon the misery of others.[86]

Kropotkin's prison experiences reinforced his political views and provided him with yet another example of the failure of social institutions premised on a traditional view of human nature. In a real sense, he saw prisons as a microcosm of bourgeois society. The prisons were overcrowded and filthy, like industrial cities. Then there was "the flagrant immorality of a corps of jailers who were practically omnipotent and whose whole function it was to terrorize and oppress the prisoners, their subjects." This was a parody of government as the lack of useful labor and the total absence of all that could contribute to the moral welfare of men was a parody of political economy.[87]

In his attack upon the theoretical foundations of orthodox penal policy Kropotkin starts with its leading idea, namely, that the penal system aims at punishing criminals. In reality, he argues, most often those hurt the most by a criminal's imprisonment are the members of his innocent family. As for the prisoner, he is in a nursery of criminal education.[88] Any remedial aspect of prison labor is nullified since one who knows he is compelled to work as a punishment must find such work revolting.[89] Prison work is slave labor and in no way resembles true work: the heartfelt need to create. The prison regime is designed to prevent the exercise of will, discretion, or any initiative. Yet life outside requires for success just these attributes.[90]

Prisons are designed to degrade the prisoner, killing the very last feelings of self-respect. The prison staff is corrupted by its authority.[91] The institution makes them petty tormentors of the prisoners, and this in turn makes the latter haters of society which the prison staff comes to personify for them.[92] Prisoners know that the thirst for riches, acquired by every possible means, is the essence of bourgeois society and that the line between the legal and illegal is hardly clear. For the inmate, jails are made for the unskillful and the unlucky.[93]

Kropotkin's preventive for crime is education of a new sort:

> ... let us assure to every child a sound education and instruction, both in manual labor and science, so as to permit him to acquire, during the first twenty years of his life, the knowledge and habits of earnest work—and we shall be in no more need of dungeons and jails, of judges and hangmen. Man is a result of those conditions in which he has grown up.[94]

Two-thirds of all breaches of law being so-called crimes against property, these will be eliminated or minimized when property, which is now the privilege of the few, is socialized. A sense of community will mitigate crime and aggression. In Western industrial cities ties between inhabitants are virtually nonexistent and the family structure disintegrates. Man should not and need not live in isolation. Interpersonal bonds will ultimately inculcate mutual support, mutual dependency, and greater equality.[95] Yet there would still remain even in anarchist society the crime of those with mental and physical diseases. Kropotkin urges that fraternal care and liberty are the best treatment for those so afflicted.[96]

CHAPTER 4

A Critical Assessment of Kropotkin's World-View

I   On Nature and the Nature of Human History

K ROPOTKIN'S view of nature has been characterized as having three major components: organic or holistic, historic, and spontaneous. In Bob Galois's schema the organic component is the most important. By organic Galois means that Kropotkin views man as a part of nature and so both subject to, and a participant in, the same processes which are operative in the rest of nature. It follows that nature is an interrelated whole and that the actions of any part make sense only in terms of their position in relation to the whole. Kropotkin often illustrates these two aspects by means of an organismic or biological analogy. Nature or some subsystem within it is described by analogy to a living organism. This mode of explication supports and in turn is supported by the recognition of growth and development in nature. Nature is historicized, and this dimension Galois believes is contained within the organic view of nature.[1]

Kropotkin follows Darwin, who was the first to place man firmly in the living world of nature. In *Mutual Aid* and *Ethics*, Kropotkin's point of departure is the animal world, where competition and cooperation are in contention. These two forces operate throughout our unique nature, extending into human society.[2]

Kropotkin stresses the interrelatedness of society. Yet he also recognizes that there are atomistic forces at work in it, especially in a capitalist society. The division of labor creates barriers to human satisfaction and to humane personal relationships; it truncates the individual. Kropotkin advocates integration and organic structuring of society through cooperation. To do this he

113

requires political economy to stress needs or consumption, instead of deeds or production.[3]

The historic aspect of nature for Kropotkin also begins with the animal world. Man is and always has been a social species. He has evolved through four stages: primitive or savage, barbarian, urban, and the state. As Galois notes, this statement in itself tells one nothing of the dynamic of history, or the operative processes of development.[4] It is substantially different from the Marxian schema of primitive communism, slave, feudal, capitalist, and socialist stages. We must look to Kropotkin's antinomies of competition and cooperation whose opposition fuels the motor of history.[5] Kropotkin's elaboration of these principles into historical forces does not necessarily lay claim to the resolution of their conflict. Still, his ascription of morality to naturalistic origins tends to render it an "organic necessity," a universal law of evolution.[6]

For Galois, the "spontaneous" dimension of Kropotkin's nature has three aspects: progress, freedom, and feeling. Clearly, in line with Kropotkin's view of the antinomial process of history, progress cannot be uniform but is rather a refractive advance through time. Advances are the fruit of spontaneity in the sense of creative activity or free evolution. Spontaneity clearly implies cooperation and is also closely related to the concept of freedom which must be socially and not individually defined. The freedom to starve is not freedom, and each individual is free only in proportion to the freedom of others. Galois's insistence on holism seems justified.

The ideal basis of society would be myriad numbers of free constructs or agreement between individuals and groups, freely made. Feeling comes into play as the irrational element in nature, the poetry of nature, that which defies delimitation or definitiveness. It is akin to the people's spirit or enthusiasm, the transcendence of vulgar materialism. Galois notes that Kropotkin recognizes the importance of nonpurposive behavior: play not only performs a social function in learning, it is an expression of the "joy of life." Human society, in sum, is a function of spontaneous or free initiative in a social milieu.[7]

For Kropotkin, the highest law for man is progress, which is defined in terms of historical advance toward the maximally happy life. From this law Kropotkin derives the demands of justice and energetic activity. I. Grossman Roshchin, a socialist and admirer, criticizes Kropotkin's formula as objectively immeasurable. How does one define the maximally possible happiness? Is this not a return to utopian socialism?[8]

Grossman-Roshchin is aware that Kropotkin's energetic activity is in pursuit of the good of the species, not of selfish pleasure,[9] but is still unsatisfied with "mutual aid": the analysis of human behavior cannot be founded on a formless, undifferentiated concept which fails to distinguish between self-interest and love.[10]

Moreover, the mechanics of the historical process remain outside of Kropotkin's attention. Everything reduces to the clash between the state principle and that of free mass creativity.[11] These forces tend to function descriptively rather than as concepts within a theoretical system. Kropotkin has no theory of history. And he does not account for the historical distortions and fettering of the streams of mass creativity. Kropotkin never deals with the Dostoevskian psychological problem of the masses — bread versus freedom. He bypasses the basic problem of sociology, the transindividual character of social phenomena. He is utterly preoccupied with the problem of good and evil in history.[12]

The anarchist critic Aleksei Borovoi locates the heart of Kropotkin's world-view in the creative role of the masses. Although Kropotkin stresses the social process rather than the "atomized individual," he is unable to conceptualize sociological laws; the masses for him are not an historically defined, ethnographically discrete reality but an amorphous, almost mystical, combination of instinct and rationality — the final repositors of creative force. And their constructs are never wrong![13]

Social antagonism is underplayed. Kropotkin's insistence on the ultimate reduction of human personality and behavior to social relations lends him to ignore the problems and conflict between individual and collective. By hypothesizing mutual aid as the dominant principle of human nature he justifies his ahistorical idealization of the people and finesses a full examination of the concrete sources of human conduct. The derivation of an organic community from the biological principle that any individual plant or animal is a federation of organs[14] remains a lose analogy. Kropotkin magnifies the role of the individual in the social process and overestimates the current

ability of the masses to assume the high technical and ethical
levels upon which the successful anarchist society must rest. By
hypothesizing the state into a metaphysical force of evil, the
masses are not only not inculpated but are granted the equally
metaphysical role of creative opposition. We are still left,
according to Borovoi, with the untidy problem of the degenera-
tion of "free" societies and a naive idealization of tribal
organization and medieval cities which Kropotkin subsumes
under the federalist principle of his biological metaphor.[15] It is
undeniable that the European urban commune of the tenth and
eleventh centuries provides a consistently lyric *leitmotif*
throughout Kropotkin's writing.[16] In the fraternity of the guild,
he sees the instinct of mutual aid socially incarnate. The passage
concludes with characteristic historical sweep.[17]

Liberty, self-administration, and peace were the chief goals of
the medieval cities. And labor was their chief foundation. But the
medieval economist was not merely production oriented. With
his practical mind, says Kropotkin, medieval man understood
that consumption must be guaranteed in order to obtain
production: therefore to provide food and lodging for the
common folk was the fundamental principle in each city.
Necessities were a first charge on all production.[18]

The legacy of the medieval cities to civilization has been
immense. They were a force against theocracy and despotism;
they endowed history with splendid examples of the variety, the
self-reliance, the force of initiative, and the immense intellectual
and material energies which is our common inheritance. But why
did they decline and fall? In good measure, offers Kropotkin,
because of the combination of the church in the service of new
would-be centralizing Caesars, together with cultural divisive-
ness among the older and newer burghers and the feuds and
rivalries between the city proper and its surrounding villages.
Even more important, perhaps, was the neglect of agriculture in
favor of commerce and industry and the ideological force of
centralization and authority, a belief in one man's power. All this
annihilated federalism, and the very creative genius of the
masses died out.[19] Never before or since, concluded Kropotkin,
has mankind known a period of relative well-being for all as in
the cities of the Middle Ages: "The poverty, insecurity, and
physical exploitation of labor that exist in our times were then
unknown."[20]

Kropotkin is sensitive to the accusation that his glorification of the communes and the Middle Ages overlooks their conflicts and domestic struggles and wars. Kropotkin argues that conflict, if it involves free debate, without resorting to outside force, and if in defense of individual liberty and the federation principle, must be distinguished from states' wars which entail the destruction of these liberties and principles; there is historically progressive and historically regressive struggle.[21] Unfortunately, no litmus tests are available to those who fail to divine the differences *a priori!*

No less an authority on the subject of medieval society than the historian Marc Bloch casts doubt upon some of Kropotkin's historical characterizations. Speaking of the communes Bloch has this to say:

Certainly these primitive urban groups were in no sense democratic. The "greater Bourgeois," who were their real founders and whom the lesser bourgeois were not always eager to follow, were often, in their treatment of the poor, hard masters and merciless creditors. But by substituting for the promise of obedience, paid for by protection, the promise of mutual aid, they contributed to the social life of Europe a new element, profoundly alien to the feudal spirit properly so-called.[22]

Kropotkin's vision of the guild's as the apotheosis of brotherhood is challenged by Stenton, who emphasizes their exclusionary policies.[23] But, for Kropotkin, the theophany of mutual aid is by no means visited on medieval Europe alone. Kropotkin preached the irrepressibility of the instinct of mutual aid. Even with the crushing power of the centralized state and the existence of the full apparatus of the competitive ideology, manifestations of the indomitable spirit of human solidarity emerge. In a typical passage he points to the integrated European railroad system.[24] Scattered liberally throughout his writings are also references to voluntary citizen groups—rescue teams, lifeboat associations, child-care groups, sports associations, etc.—all of which not only affirm the ever-present tendency toward mutual aid but which allegedly indicate an historical direction away from statism. Thomas Masaryk notes that Kropotkin forgot that international postal treaties are regulated and guaranteed by the state.[25] Alexander Gray does not see the state as having relinquished any significant functions to private individuals at the time Kropotkin was writing or since.

In fact, argues Gray, voluntary associations do not relieve the state of its functions. Rather, if they are of the right kind, they prepare the way for further extensions of state activity.[26]

Kropotkin's anarchist comrade Errico Malatesta attributes his penchant for finding theoretically reinforcing data in the weakest of evidence to his compulsively systematic personality, his tendency to explain everything with one principle, to reduce diversity to unity even at the expense of logic despite his devotion to rational modes of thought. In Malatesta's view Kropotkin:

> ... lacked that something which goes to make a true man of science: the capacity to forget one's aspirations and preconceptions and observe facts with cold objectivity. ... His normal procedure was to start with a hypothesis and then look for the facts that would confirm it—which may be a good method for discovering new things; but what happened, and quite unintentionally, was that he did not see the ones which invalidated his hypothesis.[27]

A recent student of anachism, Derry Novak strikes an appropriate balance between Kropotkin's overall views and his virtues as an historian:

> Although anthropologists and historians would not agree with Kropotkin's thesis in its entirety, owing to its emphasis on selected actors, his analysis nevertheless suggests a trend which every social science must study and which in modern times both individual and social psychology attempt to analyze and explain.[28]

II   Kropotkin's Anarcho-Communism

Kropotkin's belief in the triumph of a just, egalitarian society flowed out of a moral imperative which constituted man's evolutionary destiny. In contrast Marx's basis of history was grounded in economic arrangements interacting with objective needs; a "mode of production" was defined and limited by its inherent contradictions. The bearer of the revolution was for Kropotkin the faceless creative masses, who most definitely were not restricted to the Marxian proletariat. Kropotkin's hero was not an economic category but an amorphous creative force— collective heir to history.

In spite of anarchism's biological mandate, Kropotkin never

succeeds in convincing himself of the inevitable victory of the biologically stronger, altruistic impulse over antisocial drives. The best evidence is his constant, intense emphasis upon the importance of moral motivation for social development. As an anarchist admirer, Rudolf Rocker, points out, justice for Kropotkin has nothing in common with the metaphysical absolutes of philosophers or with any absolute laws. For Kropotkin, the feeling of justice in man is a natural result of social coexistence and common strivings which unite people: a social dynamic and an ongoing instinctual force. Time and circumstance strongly influence the human will. But neither time, economic circumstances, nor social conditions can guarantee man deliverance. What is absolutely necessary is a profound moral commitment to create a socialist society. In contrast to this appeal to the whole personality, Marxian economic analysis transforms the empirical individual into the concept of labor, an input into the machine of social production.[29] Typically anarchist, Kropotkin sees in the phenomenon of personal emotions the highest expression of the instinct of freedom in man, an instinct which takes precedence over any "objective" necessity.[30] For Kropotkin the "person" is prior to class consciousness or economically based political viewpoints.

Yet another point of distinction between Marx and Kropotkin is methodology. Kropotkin claims to base his social investigations and conclusions exclusively on what he calls the inductive-deductive method of the natural sciences. He is extremely hostile to the dialectical method of Marx. For Kropotkin political economy is a material science, the physiology of society.[31] Kropotkin sees Marx's work as another variant of Hegelian metaphysics.[32] In fact, according to Martin A. Miller, Kropotkin holds tenaciously to a view of Marx as a fraudulent thinker firmly rooted in the tradition of utopian socialism. Despite the coincidence of their views that progress emerges out of the resolution of conflict in both nature and society, Kropotkin's assumptions about the genesis, modes, and forms of resolution are quite un-Marxian.

Kropotkin's economics start with needs, not production: political economy is to study the best means of satisfying all present needs with the least expenditure of energy. For Kropotkin production is always a means to an end, not an end in itself. He asks: Does man exist for the economy or the economy

for man? Kropotkin reaches a conclusion not shared by most
socialists of his time: far more is being produced under the
existent economic system than needed by the population. He sets
out to prove that uncritical faith in the necessity of the division
of labor and industrial centralization as essentials for efficient
and sufficient production is wrong. He attempts to show how the
amount of labor can be reduced and the nature of work changed
into a more human form without threatening subsistence but
rather with resulting increases in efficiency and human satisfaction. His answer is decentralization of industry and the integration rather than the division of labor. This is his economic road to
socialism.[33]

Kropotkin, in attacking wage or hired labor in any form,
attacks the idea that one can justifiably evaluate or measure
labor according to its value to society. He decries as arbitrary the
distinction between skilled or unskilled labor. The fascination
with relating an objective cost of production to labor time is, for
Kropotkin, a fetish of Marx and of classic political economy—a
fruitless abstraction without any scientific basis. Exchange value
and the quantity of labor are not commensurate. Kropotkin does
not object to Adam Smith's idea that the exchange value of a
good increases with the growth of the quantity of labor
expended on its production but reasons that to draw the
conclusion that in consequence the two things are proportional,
that one is the measure of the other, is a gross mistake.[34]

Kropotkin's anarchist-communism flows out of two sources: on
the one hand, from his study of economics and history, and on the
other, from his moral ideas of equality and freedom. He
considers his insistence on the abolition of a wage system and of
all differences in the payment and evaluation of labor
historically justified. Means of production— technological and
intellectual—are the products of past and present social labor.
Kropotkin argues that it is not production costs but the monopoly
over culture and education which creates colossal inequality in
social relations. Knowledge constitutes a distinct form of capital
which exploits more fundamentally than any other. The higher
pay of the skilled is very simply a matter of perpetuating the
advantage of some at the expense of others. It is no more natural
to measure a share of social wealth than to distinguish between
goods of consumption and of production. All products are social
property. Here Kropotkin's position must be opposed to

Bakunin's platform of "each entitled to the full product of his labor." In insisting that any system of distribution is artificial, anarchist–communism transcends Bakunist collectivism. And it is the former which, at least by the 1880s, was to largely represent the goals of the anarchist movement.

Moral as well as historic vision animates Kropotkin's economic quarrels. That classic political economy, from Smith through Marx, should give production pride of place with a derivative role for individual needs can only be repugnant to Kropotkin. The precedence of need is not merely a question of separating the right to life, to collective goods from participation in productive labor; it provides a political principle as well: equality of all, denial of power to any. No measure of relative worth can be justified. Above all, human need represents the highest evolution of human history. Need must be the starting point of any social analysis; the free unfolding of human potential must be the end and the sustaining vision of the anarchist future.

III   *Federalism*

Kropotkin holds as sacred the principle of association based on free agreement between completely independent individuals or groups, be they revolutionary organizations or postrevolutionary communes. The complement of free agreement is "mutual" or "collective responsibility": the work responsibility of each to his society. At least one anarchist sympathizer, Peter Arshinov, claims that Kropotkin himself in 1920 acknowledged the practical failure of this federalist social form with the demise of the Russian anarchist movement.[35] Arshinov criticized Kropotkin from the vantage point of the Bolshevik consolidation and its destruction of the anarchists. He called for an anarchist party to lead a Makhno-type partisan army premised on ruthless class struggle undiluted by vague Kropotkinian notions of supra-class species mutual aid and cooperation. Kropotkin's utopian vision was no substitute for a realistic plan of defending the revolution in a period of civil war. The organizational question had to be resolved and Kropotkin's reliance on spontaneous free association was a bar to any anarchist victory hopes.[36] Another sympathetic student, Camillo Berneri, considers federalism, though hardly a systematic theory, one of the most interesting aspects of his political thought.[37] Berneri concludes:

In Kropotkin's Federalism there is excessive optimism, there are simplifications and contradictions, but there is also a great truth: that freedom is a condition of life and development for all people: that only where a people governs itself and for itself is it safe from the scourge of tyranny and certain of its progress.[38]

Vincent C. Punzo sees Kropotkin's criticism of the state as a means of articulating such political values as liberty and justice; his call for the replacement of the state by a system of federated communities is an instrument for realizing such values.[39] Kropotkin insists that the state, understood as a hierarchical, centralized structure directing the lives of its citizens, is by its very nature inimical to the humanitarian ideals it claims to serve. Kropotkin employs the principle that a social institution is to be understood by the direction in which it has developed. How can the state function as a servant of society while coercing individuals to obey it? Its hierarchical structure is its essential characteristic, and this is destructive of the communal life it claims to serve and which is necessary to realize freedom and equality. It deprives its citizens of the type of environment which human beings need to develop a sense of shared interests and responsibilities. Effective decisions become the monopoly of the few.[40] The structure of state existence contributes to the development of a mind set and life-style that places matters of public business beyond the scope of citizens' responsibilities.[41] As for the federated communes, they are only the rough draft of an ideal because Kropotkin, says Punzo, recognizes the futility of trying to present a detailed blueprint of the future.[42] Nonetheless, Punzo sees in federation the sketch of an alternative communitarian individualism opposed to the predatory egoism of bourgeois society which, in fact, stunts individual initiative and growth.

Kropotkin's analyses are contrasted with what Punzo calls "bureaucratic realism." Social evils are seen as aberrations—so many pimples on the body politic. Punzo believes that contemporary political thinking has become so enamored of the remedies of bureaucratic realism that instead of trying to find a remedy that suits the full depth and seriousness of certain problems, it recognizes as problems only those areas that can be treated by its remedies.[43] This is an appropriate rejoinder to those incrementalists who glibly affix the stigma of utopian to any fundamental social criticism.

A far more significant challenge to Kropotkin, according to Punzo, is structural realism. It argues that the conditions under which people presently exist render the possibilities for a free communal existence empty abstractions. Punzo cites Robert Heilbroner, who sympathizes with Kropotkin's political goals but finds them unrealistic within the present historical context. Punzo adds that this conclusion raises the ironic possibility that Kropotkin's anarchist communism must be rejected as a perspective because the modern state has been much more effective in destroying the communal resources of human existence than Kropotkin realized. Yet he concludes on a most Kropotkinian note of hope in the active role of human consciousness:

> Thus, so long as there is the slightest reason to doubt Heilbroner's prediction, we would do well to probe as thoroughly as possible for a type of social order in which all members can play a direct and significant part in the determination of public policy. . . . Kropotkin's critique of state existence and defense of the possibility of a communitarian existence provide a useful generalized perspective wherein such a probing into our present situation can be conducted.[44]

IV *Penology and Social Control*

Kropotkin views mutual aid as the most effective tool against antisocial behavior and advocates that society should shift from a primarily punitive to a primarily preventive approach to antisocial behavior. This means primary attention must be directed to the underlying cause of aberrant behavior. While Kropotkin grants that inherited tendencies may play a minor role in causing some criminal action, the primary causative factor is the role of social structure. The issue of the practicality of autonomous internalized social controls over antisocial behavior, be it criminal in the traditional sense or merely egoistic self-seeking or self-indulgence, is critical to the communitarian lifestyle. Emile Capouya and Keitha Tomkins consider Kropotkin's penological views far in advance of what now goes by the name of enlightened penology:

> Having noticed that the great majority of prisoners come from one social class, and that their number can be accurately predicted from year to year, it was clear to him that the existence of that class was the true ground of antisocial action. . . . What scientific prejudice looked upon as natural and inevitable, the concentration of bad bloodlines in

the poorest class, Kropotkin saw as a comforting illusion. The conditions of life to which that class was subjected could amply explain the incidence of crime within it.[45]

Writings by contemporary Western Marxist criminologists tend to agree with Kropotkin's analysis of the social causes of crime without completely sharing his faith in internalized individual or group controls in the post revolutionary society. This viewpoint implicitly calls into question what it would style the oversimplified Kropotkinian view of the state as a crude repression-machine in favor of a far more multi-faceted approach to its role as the primary creator-enforcer of bourgeois ideology.

Jack Young opines that no one can imagine the disappearance of control in any society, but that this control can be democratized, informalized, and need not involve the near-irrevocable stigmatization which it involves in present-day capitalist society. In an advanced socialist society the problem of control—as Kropotkin emphasized—would be greatly diminished.[46]

Frank Pierce considers the distinction between the "imaginary" and the "real" social orders of Western capitalist societies fundamental to understanding the actual *modus operandi* of the repressive apparatus. The "imaginary social order" presents these societies as having been freely chosen via the democratic processes, as having a free-enterprise system humanized by elements of a mixed economy. The "real social order" is a monopoly capitalist system with a certain degree of state control of the industrial infrastructure but where the state itself is ultimately dominated by the ruling class. The crucial point is that the system is not maintained by force alone. The legitimating functions of the imaginary social order are important and profound; legal statutes are but one very formalized expression of the "rules" regulating social life. Such rules, says Pierce, are communicated and institutionalized in the everyday practices of ordinary people through the ideological apparatus. They are important for the maintenance of the attitudes and focus of life compatible with capitalism.[47]

This view would be backed by philosopher Martin Buber. Buber suggests that Kropotkin's target should not have been the state as such but only the existing order in all its forms. His anarchy is in reality "anocracy," that is, not the absence of government but the absence of domination.[48] Buber feels that Kropotkin, like Bakunin, misses the all-important fact that, in the social as opposed to the political sphere, revolution can only perfect, set free, and lend its stamp of authority to something that has already been foreshadowed in the womb of the prerevolutionary society. The revolutionary moment is one of birth, not begetting.[49] And the state is not, as Kropotkin thought, an institution which can be destroyed by a revolution. Rather it is a relationship between people, a mode of behavior which only can be replaced by another.[50]

Kropotkin would seem to have underrated the subtlety of the web of loyalties and symbols—the coherence of the sign system which constitutes the ideological (meta) language of capitalism. He concentrates his energy and his analysis on state bureaucracies rather than on the attitude-molding and attitude-manufacturing institutions, the *"appareils ideologiques"* which do not substantially reduce to the state administrative structure.

The implications are clear: deep roots are not easily extirpated even by a great revolutionary explosion of spontaneous origin ignited by the untutored, creative masses. Social demolition, while hardly as easy as Bakunin imagined, is truly separated from construction by an immense gulf, and reeducation in the new morality, no mean feat in itself, is hardly more than a starting point in transforming actual conduct on a social scale. Creating new roots, albeit that the delicate runners of mutual aid are already there, is no overnight job. Kropotkin's disallowance of any form of government for some ill-defined transitional period would mean leaving the rebuilding to myriad numbers of small communes. A thousand flowers may bloom, but they would not necessarily agree on a working definition of mutual aid or necessarily waltz in step.

Just what would be the limits of diversity, the means and form of social coherence? Richard Sennett believes that as a result of the adolescent identity crisis, men become accomplices in their own social adaptation through a desire for a controlled, purified experience which makes them feel threatened by ambiguity and uncertainty and resistant to new experiences and ideas. Simply abolishing the present system will not lead to a millennial flowering.[51] Aggression, regardless of origin, is important in man's activities, and a society that regards its outbreak as a hindrance rather than a serious human experience is hiding from itself.[52] For Sennett a modern system of ethics does not advocate the practice of goodness for its own sake which ultimately tends to self-righteous and intolerant ends but rather must make an ethical condition spontaneously and unconsciously emerge from social situations.[53] Sennett feels that the disorder of large, modern cities, a living anarchy, provides, in contrast to the Kropotkinian village community, a milieu favoring tolerance and intellectual stimulation. Out of the clash of diversities will come an order imposed by the actors themselves.[54] Similar allegations of the repressive and depressing homogeneity of small communities are raised by such liberal or libertarian spokesmen as Buber and Eric Hobsbawn.

On the issue of the necessity of external social controls, Marxists attack Kropotkin's stateless postrevolutionary schema on the basis that authority and power to enforce it are necessary to protect society from antisocial inclinations. The division of labor is still necessary and must be enforced. This assumption that behavior must be imposed on men by an outside authority is attacked by the Kropotkinian John Hewetson as a premise which makes the erection of a central coercive authority a logical necessity in the face of the biological mandate of mutual aid in all human and animal societies. Hewetson reaffirms the Kropotkinian faith, without qualification, as most practical and realistic: "The necessity for an authority to "restrain the structural egoism of the individual" is simply illusory, and a product of capitalist ideology."[55]

Still, Kropotkin's reliance on the socially cohesive principle of labor voluntarily shared by members of the federation, his crucial assumption of spontaneous social behavior from men as "working animals"—has been criticized from all points of the ideological spectrum as naive, overly optimistic, unsound psychologically.

George Bernard Shaw, a personal admirer of Kropotkin's and a Fabian socialist, wrote that Kropotkin had too optimistic a view of the average man. Shaw thought Kropotkin's vision of man as a fallen angel rather useless:

If the fallacies of absolute morality are to be admitted in the discussion at all, he must be considered rather as an obstinate and selfish devil, who is being slowly forced by the iron tyranny of Nature to recognize that in disregarding his neighbor's happiness he is taking the surest way to sacrifice his own. . . . The practical question remains, could men trained under our present system be trusted to pay for their food scrupulously if they could take it for nothing with impunity? Clearly, if they did not so pay, anarchist-communism would be bankrupt in two days. ... I do not deny the possibility of the final attainment of that degree of moralization; but I contend that the path to it lies through a transition system which, instead of offering fresh opportunities to men of getting their living idly, will destroy those opportunities altogether, and wean us from the habit of regarding such an anomaly as possible, much less desirable.[56]

A fellow socialist of the following generation looks at the anarchist-communist distribution by need and noncompulsory work principles in greater depth. Bertrand Russell asks whether it is technically possible to provide the necessities of life in such large quantities as would be needed if every man and woman could take as much of them from the public stores as they might desire. He believes that the principle of unlimited supply could be adopted in regard to all communities for which the demand has limits that fall short of what can be easily produced. But it requires efficient production. Thus, as he sees it, there is no technical impossibility in the free sharing schemes. But he asks whether the necessary work would be done if the individual were assured of the general standard of comfort even though he did no work. Russell comments that the great bulk of necessary work can never be anything but painful or at least painfully monotonous. Special privileges will have to be accorded those who undertake it. Doing this need not create any vital breach in the anarchist system. If hours could be drastically reduced and if the workers were given a self-management role, most could be brought to prefer productive labor to idleness, even men whose bare livelihood would be assured whether they worked or not. As to the rest, special rewards could be given out to those who undertook it. The certain proportion of the population that preferred idleness, provided it was small, need not matter.[57]

But Russell, who regards freedom as the greatest of political goods—not the greatest of goods—feels that respect for the liberty of others is not a natural impulse with men. If all men's actions were wholly unchecked by external authority, the strong would oppress the weak, the majority the minority, and the more violent the more peaceable. He feels, like Shaw, that aggressive behavior is not wholly due to social structure, though he concedes that the present competitive organization of society does a great deal to foster the worst in human nature. Although community mores can make cruelty rare, formal law is needed.[58] So long as the love of power exists, he sees no way of preventing it from finding an outlet in oppression except by means of the organized force of the community.

For Russell the state seems a necessary institution for certain purposes—peace, war, regulation of sanitary conditions, tariffs, etc.—which could hardly be performed in a community without central government.[59] Skeptical of direct, participatory democracy, April Carter further elaborates on the necessity of government to deal with the complexities of an urban and industrial society and especially with the coordination required by long-term economic planning.[60]

Three final commentators are included because of the interest of their systematic, more or less theoretically directed critique as opposed to the disparate impressions of common sense. Leader of a shortlived 1968 Dutch anarchist group, Roel van Duyn bases his anticapitalism on Kropotkin's views and values. His criticism is methodological. Van Duyn feels Kropotkin's "positivism" and rejection of dialectics leads to an impoverishment and hypostatization of the categories of authority and adaptation, aggression and cooperation. The psychological bond between oppressor and victim, the mutuality of social and aggressive instincts powered by a single force—"the current alternating between attraction and repulsion between those complementary poles"—remains unexplored.[61]

Barrington Moore, Sr., writes from a problematic which redefines the object of historical analysis. Leaving aside an anthropology of human needs or human nature, Moore focuses on the efficacy of social relations. His critique is directed at anarchism in general but the questions raised are pertinent to Kropotkin's federalism. Moore poses the problem of just how independent anarchist communities can be expected to get along with each other. He sees community rivalries deriving not from any inherent feature of human nature but from the organizational form of autonomous political units. It is social organization, not scarcity, which imposes a power drive. What would be the consequence of some communities controlling resources that others require? How can the spontaneous emergence of market relations from independent production and political units be checked and replaced by other social bonds? In their absence, would such a restrictive moral code be necessary and would it cast a repressive miasma over the whole culture?[62]

Aileen Kelly reflects what might be styled a "macro-critical" approach. Kropotkin's historical, biological, sociological studies reflect the naively messianic and teleological ideologies of his time. The theory of instinctual mutual aid is a new version of the ancient myth of primal innocence; the distinction between the drive to solidarity as the "law" of man's nature and the drive to domination as a corruption of nature is theological dualism in modern dress. Kropotkin, like Marx, constructs a secular eschatology.

Kelly cites the "empirical" evidence of history against Kropotkin's romantic nostalgia for "barbarian freedom" and primitive communism: "No empirical method can demonstrate that human individuality which, throughout history, has been experienced only in relations of dependence on society and tension with it, is destined to perfect itself through perfect identification with the social whole, or that a technologically sophisticated economy will reach ultimate perfection by reverting to the primitive democracy and the total integration of functions characterizing early communal existence."[63] But Kelly's empiricism is itself grounded in something akin to the symbolic language of myth—an existential human condition reminiscent of the view of Herzen and perhaps Camus. She sees historical progress generated by tension between the eternal categories of individual and social environment. Attempts at a synthesis or resolution can only impose the dogmatism of systematization on the very essence of life and creativity: the conflict between conservation and utopia, aspiration for and negation of the absolute. It is not surprising then that, for Kelly, Kropotkin's nihilist consistency is his most important legacy to the European left. Almost alone in his uncomprising aversion to the *real politik* of end justifying means, Kropotkin is able to maintain that most difficult of political postures: a delicate balance between faith and skepticism in an always imperfectly realized ideal.

We might end on a prosaic note from contemporary Russia. In the eyes of the present regime Kropotkin stands condemned as *petit bourgeois*:[64] he champions small-scale production, claims a statist form of property engenders state capitalism, stoops to a

Bakuninist orientation toward the peasant masses. The list of heresies runs from Spencerian evolutionism to support of the Makhno movement during the Civil War.[65]

The poverty of official Soviet philosophy need not concern us here. But it is certain that the "bad marks" of the Soviet apologists leave the challenge of Kropotkin's lyrical faith in a humane future unscathed.

V *Kropotkin's Economics: The Whole and the Parts*

Errico Malatesta put forward a crucial criticism of Kropotkin's economics shared by some anarchists, Marxists, and capitalists. Kropotkin had accepted the idea that the accumulated stock of food and manufactured goods was so abundant that for a long time to come it would not be necessary to worry about production; the immediate problem was one of consumption; for the triumph of the revolution it was necessary to satisfy the needs of everyone immediately as well as abundantly. Production would follow the rhythm of consumption.[66]

Malatesta may have erred in assuming that scarcity is likely to be a permanent feature of human society; Kropotkin's belief that ongoing technology would overcome scarcity has gained credibility over time. In challenging the primacy of consumption, however, Malatesta does raise an important issue: how can Kropotkin's myriad near-autarkies meet the challenge of creating a system of extended reproduction?

For Kropotkin, of course, there can be no doubt of the advantages — political, productive, and normative — of the small-scale, autonomous economic unit. This form of economic decentralization is to function as the analogue of federalist political autonomy. Kropotkin imputes the advance under capitalism of large centralized production units to a cheap supply of unskilled labor rather than to any necessary economies of scale. Once the wage relationship is eliminated, workers' cooperatives as small as technologically feasible can optimize production, especially of finished goods; only standardized intermediate products need be mass produced. More important, the human scale of the workshop can make possible a democratic and participatory system of self-management. Rejuvenating a tradition of craftsmanship will suppress the minute subdivision of the capitalist labor process and the stultifying effect of factory discipline for the individual worker. On the international level, Kropotkin charges the division of labor with tending toward imperialist rivalry and war and he shows enough clairvoyance to focus on the economic relations of dependence between industrial powers and rural satellites condemned to monoculture geared to export. Indeed, so close is Kropotkin to advocating autarky that he seems mistrustful of any foreign trade.[67] Self-sufficiency, especially in food production, must be the goal of industrialized and rural areas alike. This is to be achieved by intensifying cultivation through radical agrarian and industrial decentralization. The application of science to agriculture will increase yields, but the use of chemicals is rejected as too costly in favor of organic farming. Small work units are to function at the point of production within "humanly scaled" autonomous communities which seem to combine an economic and a political personality. Economically, these communities may be described as agro-industrial combines which regulate output according to the needs of a local market.

The pertinence of such a "model" for economies characterized by a low-level of industrialization and a large underemployed peasantry is twofold: development of what Marxists would call the productive forces is to be achieved through reallocation of cooperative labor and reorganization of the work process itself rather than through massive accumulation or through a choice of agricultural techniques heavily dependent on an industrialized sector and on a high level of energy inputs.

For Emile Capouya and Keitha Tompkins, Kropotkin's focus on the national and international division of labor has yielded insights equally relevant to "advanced" industrial societies. From the perspective of economic and social analysis, Kropotkin demonstrates the linkage of the Malthusian demographic profile with capitalist domination of the world market. On a normative level, his critique of early forms of industrial organizations is too farsighted to have found the requisite points of leverage in that stage of capitalism. Only now are the human contradictions of socialism and capitalism alike sufficiently developed to correspond to Kropotkin's criticism.[68]

For Kropotkin, of course, such praise would be at least faintly damning. He was not interested in disembodied value judgments and wavered between the belief and the fervent hope that his principles of economic decentralization and self-sufficiency would in fact find material levers within society. A sympathetic socialist commentator, G. D. H. Cole, stresses that Kropotkin's bitter protest against capitalist industrial organization is neither Luddite nor romantically antitechnological. [69] History is to side with the decentralization, not in spite of, but with the aid of mechanization.

Here, it is Kropotkin's critics who are likely to find historical leverage. Particularly trenchant is Max Nettlau, a prominent historian of the anarchist movement, who not only claims that the inequality between fragmented communities is divisive and inimical to anarchism but that such fragmentation runs counter to the spirit and tendencies of the period 1880–1930. Socialism, according to Nettlau, strives for universality and solidarity; Kropotkin stands for the industrial-agrarian atomization of mankind. [70] On this ringing note, we might hear from another critic, no less formidable a centralist than Joseph Stalin, who has this to say about the feasibility of Kropotkin's economic projections:

... the economic development of the capitalist system shows that present-day production is expanding day after day. It is not confined within the limits of individual towns and provinces, but constantly overflows these limits and spreads over the whole country. Consequently, we must welcome the expansion of production and regard as the basis of future socialism not separate towns and communities but the entire indivisible territory of the whole state which, in future, will, of course, expand more and more. And this means that the doctrine advocated by Kropotkin, which confines future socialism within the limits of separate towns and communities, is a hindrance to the powerful expansion of production; it is harmful to the proletariat. [71]

Stalin's critique is amplified and elaborated on by the contemporary Soviet student of anarchism, F. Ia. Polianskii, who criticizes Kropotkin for equating the international division of labor with colonialism. It will and should survive the demise of colonialism because economic specialization of geographical zones raises the productivity of production and lowers costs. [72] More fundamental than Stalin's criticism, Polianskii argues that Kropotkin's starting point for economic analysis, consumption, ignores the fact that only if productive forces are sufficiently ripe can consumption stimulate production. Kropotkin is accused of echoing the Austrian school of Böhm-Bawerk, Wieser and

Menger, according to which value is defined by its usefulness to the purchaser, that is by the reaction of the individual to it in terms of the fulfilment of his needs as he perceives them.[73] This is the subjectivist approach to value. Polianskii credits Kropotkin with having pioneered the Trotskyist notion that the nationalization of production leads to the triumph of state capitalism since Marxism after the revolution preserves hired labor, wages and distribution according to the quantity and quality of work. Kropotkin opposed the idea of a greater reward for skilled labor, which Polianskii labels sheer demagoguery since differential rewards under socialism encourages acceleration of technical progress and growth of labor productivity in a context where the acquisition of skills is open to all.[74] Kropotkin, while indisputably a revolutionary, was not a communist. He believed the advantages of huge production were problematical. Like Bakunin, he was in essence a bourgeois individualist, a communalist not a communist.[75] His acceptance of the application of machines was predicted on their not undermining the basis of petty goods production.[76] His anarchist-communism was bourgeois individualism "turned inside out."[77]

Kropotkin's contribution to solving the agrarian problem is denigrated by Polianskii. He indiscriminately viewed the problems of feudal Russia with those of semi-capitalist and capitalist Western European countries, mistakenly supposing that agrarian programs should be identical in all countries independently of their respective levels of development and the character of their social structures.[78] More importantly, the idealized voluntary peasant commune which he championed as the model for rural transformation precluded industrialization. How can intensification occur so as to provide the chemical fertilizers upon which Kropotkin premised his hopes for major increases in crop yields on without huge chemical plants to produce them? And Kropotkin nowhere described exactly how he envisioned communal cultivation to take place other than to call for the land to go to those who work it. This would lead to ultimate inequality in land distribution. While vague on the concrete mode of cultivation he favored, he clearly doubted the worth of huge farms even in capitalist conditions. This betokens a petty production bias. In general Kropotkin, in fixating on the high productivity of intensive production, overlooked the fact that in extensive production labor productivity increases despite lower yields as a result of lower expenditures of human labor and means of production per unit of area.[79]

Stalin and Polianskii bring us full circle back to Malatesta; how and in what form will Kropotkin's communities reproduce themselves? To put it another way, how successfully has Kropotkin been able to eliminate economic contradictions conceptually in order to lay an adequate theoretical foundation for their domination by economic and political practice? At this point, we had best turn to the "dismal science" and call in the economists. We will discriminate two orders of discourse. The first deals with the economic problems of reproduction and distribution. Subtending each commentary will be assumptions as to the "place" of distribution: its autonomy relative to a system of production. Second, we will pick up on an ongoing dialogue among leftists to which Kropotkin is, in a sense, contemporary. How consonant are the political goals of participatory democracy and workers' economic control with a planned economy?

"Orthodox" economist Catherine van Dusseldorf focuses on Kropotkin's omission of the economic category of capital formation or social savings. Redistribution without adequate accumulation will regenerate both poverty and hierarchy.[80]

The socialist economic theoretician M. Tugan-Baranovsky finds a logical contradiction in Kropotkin's insistence on absolute communal equality and absolute individual freedom including the right not to work. More tellingly, Tugan-Baranovsky claims that even if an optimal ideological and political practice is granted, anarchist economic analysis is theoretically and practically inadequate. The indispensable condition for a social economy is proportionality of its component forces. This means, according to Tugan-Baranovosky, that either a market or a plan must control social production and set proportions:

> Anarchical production is conceivable only under one condition, namely: that everybody by his own personal efforts create all objects he requires, a condition which is identical with the extinction of every economic coalescence whatever and precludes *eo ipso* the necessity of establishing rules relating to the upholding of a ratio.[81]

While not disputing the formal equivalence between the rationality of a freely competitive market and that of central planning in optimizing the allocation of resources, economist Radoslav Selucky endorses the full consequences of Kropotkin's communal economic decentralization: full "rights" over disposal of products and utilization of means of production make each economic collective a proprietor in regard to all the others. Exchange must therefore be regulated by market prices. If the economic protagonists are to be the production units themselves rather than an apparatus of central planners, Selucky insists that Marx, and by implication Kropotkin, must be explicitly revised so as to accept as inevitable the role of a market. Indicative programming is allowed, but state property—which functions economically as central planning—precludes working-class economic and political control. This is for two reasons: first, without a market, the autonomy of the self-managing production unit disappears as "free" exchange is replaced by the hierarchical relations of a "command" economy; second, the central plan—and centralized bureaucracies—dethrone the consumer as sovereign of producer decisions.[82]

In the name of the authentic Marx, Hillel Ticktin picks up the gauntlet. His rebuttal of Selucky's market-Socialism garners the expected Marxian wisdom backed by the requisite citations from "Capital." Under the aegis of market exchange, communities will engage in mutual relations of exploitation and subordination; each autonomous unit will be the subject of capitalist accumulation. Monopoly, inflation, unemployment, business cycles will reemerge. The central plan—sole alternative to the self-regulatory mechanism of the market—need not function oppressively or entail a statist hierarchy. Political and ideological institutions will be assigned the role of guarantors of participatory democracy.[83]

A more illuminating perspective on Kropotkin's economic decentralization—and on the tangled problems of planning versus market regulation—may be offered by Ticktin's sometime opponent, Marxist economist Charles Bettelheim. For Bettelheim, the several elements of the productive structures (direct producer, object, means of production, nonproducer) must be conceptualized in terms of a plurality of relationships. Discrete modes of production are given by the specific forms of combination of these elements as relations of property. These relations between agents and means of production and between the agents with each other constitute the technical and social division of labor.

Bettelheim specifies the object of economic science; it is given as "the analysis of the effects of the double articulation productive forces/relations of production."[84] Since each of these categories is conceptualized as a structure (a series of relationships), there can be no question of representing "productive forces" as a physical enumeration of techniques and resources. Rather we are dealing with a variation of the "technical" (social) relations of production: that is, a form of organization of the labor process which is strictly internal to the definition of mode of production. By discriminating among these forms, Bettelheim is able to give relations of power and subordination among the agents of production an economic content:

> ... it is necessary to distinguish the different types of capacity and of power of disposal over products and means of production and, within each type, the degrees or the levels of capacity and power of disposition. ... The term "detention" of the means of production is proposed to designate the relationship of the immediate producers to certain means of production insofar as these means intervene directly in the labor process. ... By possession is designated the relationship of certain agents of production (whether or not immediate producers), and therefore of the economic units they control, to the means of production within these economic units, insofar as these agents dominate the labor process. ...[85]

What is gained by such an approach? First, the optimal size of a production or economic unit in terms of maximizing either output or workers' control cannot rationally be decided by political fiat. The unity of the material and social conditions of production (and reproduction) must be internalized by economic theory. Second, the polemic opposition of plan versus market as presented by both Selucky and Ticktin lacks economic significance without a differential analysis of each term. The question of economic relations of exploitation or equality can only be determined by the coincidence or noncoincidence of the relations of possession and detention and between the relations of "real" and "formal" appropriation. In this light, Kropotkin's faith in universal franchise (the cooperative instincts) to coordinate production or Ticktin's in political institutions to democratize planning would at the least meet the resistance of economic laws.

It is on the level of conceptualization that the inadequacy of Kropotkin's "economics" is apparent. Barring him from the brotherhood of the dismal science would doubtless bother Kropotkin not at all. And we may certainly grant him insights. The political-economic character of his agro-industrial combines is of interest as a communal form well suited to the type of "economic calculation" incorporating political and social objectives which can be effected under a socialist or transitional society. His emphasis on reorganizing the labor process rather than simply adding to productive potential is especially perceptive. But we cannot really call Kropotkin an economic theorist. The point of departure for his "economics" was never a reflection on a specific discourse as, for example, it is with Marx, who inherited as theoretical raw material the Ricardian problems of a standard of value and the relation of value production with a system of distribution. More significantly, Kropotkin is unable to produce a concept of the "economic" as an internally constituted object of analysis. His economic observations—and they are no more than that—are derivative. This charge refers not only to their foundation on a speculative anthropology of human needs but in the cruder sense of "following" political or ethical norms, biological or social analysis.

Aurel Friedmann speaks to the point here. He underscores Kropotkin's failure to theorize capitalist production—especially the wage relation and the cyclical crises. The possibility of transcending capitalism is referred to a sketched recitation of "facts," the intentions of political groups and the alleged instability of governments. Friedmann insists on the empiricist nature of Kropokin's contradictions: impressionistic observations are presented as "facts" and juxtaposed without the establishment of determinate relationships between them.[86]

Kropotkin does indeed stand accused of economic empiricism. Insofar as the business of an economist is to explain the material functioning of society, an explanation whose coherence depends on determinate social relations, Kropotkin seems equidistant from classic political economy and Marxism. Kropotkin's haste to ground quantifications in a bedrock "data language" assumes the transparency of the economy. The crudity of the calculations may underscore Kropotkin's economic naiveté even for the casual reader. But the implication here is a critique of any empiricist or positivist economics which proceeds to a direct "economic reading" without first producing the concept of the unity of the material and social conditions of production. The critique would apply not only to the theorists of subjective value but to those who see a socialist economy ceasing to function according to its own laws in order to express human creative activity.

Kropotkin, as critic of social and economic explanation, seems extraordinarily close to the Marx of the 1844 economic manuscripts, where *homo faber* producing himself through the teleological unfolding of history progressively reveals the "essence": "free, conscious activity is man's species character."

For the rest, we might end with the further irony that by his refusal to deal with the problem of an independent determination constant in the field of value theory and by focusing on consumption and distribution at the expense of production, Kropotkin tended in the direction that economic discourse takes after 1830, that is towards the marginalist school whose "values" were annihilative of his.

VI   *Kropotkin and Human Nature: Of Altruism, Aggression, and the Genes in the Light of Recent Research*

The eminent biologist George Gaylord Simpson believes man to be, as Kropotkin believed, the only ethical animal. Man consciously chooses his values. He is by biological capacity and necessity an ethicizing animal by virtue of natural selection. And, again as Kropotkin held, he is a social animal and his individualization is crucially affected by the human social environment. Dependence on society begins with the biological dependence of infant and mother.[87] Man as the ethicizing animal is also reflected in the views of the British biologist C. H. Waddington, who considers moral orders in mankind an essential function of human social organization.[88]

As to the relative weights of environment and the innate in human behavior, the nurture-nature antimony, Waddington,[89] ethologist Niko Tinbergen,[90] and geneticist Theodosius Dobzhansky agree that in biology it is not considered possible to make clear distinctions between activities or properties which are acquired or innate. All characteristics of humans emerge from the development of inborn potentialities in relation to environmental circumstances. As Dobzhansky stresses, intelligence is not merely a genetic function. Genes really determine the reaction ranges exhibited by individuals with more or less similar genes over the entire gamut of possible environments. Heredity is not a status but a process.[91] The microbiologist Rene Dubos points out that certain behavioral traits like physical and mental apathy, long assumed to have racial or climatic origins, are often a form of physiological adjustment to malnutrition. Malnutrition occurring at a critical time of brain development appears to handicap mental development almost irreversibly. Dubos goes on to make the point that chemical fluids in cells profoundly influence gene activity and thus the external environment by constantly affecting the composition of the bodily fluids. This influence can ultimately alter the activity of the genetic apparatus. Thus individual experience determines the extent to which the genetic environment is converted into functional attributes. Dubos argues powerfully for the predominance in practice of environmental stimuli in determing human conduct.[92] Clearly Kropotkin's perhaps ascientific assumptions about the fundamental educability of virtually everyone and environmental factors as the key to molding a practical ethical society based on social equality are strengthened by these findings.

Perhaps the leading student of altruism among animals is the eminent zoologist W. C. Allee, who credits Kropotkin's *Mutual Aid* with keeping the idea of cooperation alive and popularizing it, despite the doubtful scientific basis for much of this evidence,[93] a view that approximates the consensus view among ethologists.[94] Allee's experiments and data from his animal studies suggest that while both egoistic and altruistic forces exist in nature, the altruistic are biologically the more important and vital and they alone allow for the evolution from the simpler to the more complicated animals. Allee further concludes, as did Kropotkin, that human altruistic drives are firmly based on those of their animal ancestors; the lesson for the future of mankind is that a new social order based primarily on altruistic patterns, despite the existence of strong competitive, egoistic drives, is both possible, practical and necessary.[95]

The Kropotkin-Allee view is accepted in modified form by the ethologist Irenaus Eibl-Eibesfeldt, who feels that both human aggressiveness and altruism are phylogenetically based, inborn drives, although she attributes the astonishing development of human culture to cooperation. Mutual aid reaches its heights in the higher animals and man. And she denies the theory that man is by nature a killer.[96] Ethologist Robert L. Trivers, while admitting that there is no direct evidence of the genetic basis of human altruism, also feels that in the face of the extensive development of mutual aid among humans it is reasonable to assume that cooperation has been an important factor in recent human evolution and that the underlying emotional dispositions affecting altruistic behavior have important genetic components.[97]

Garrett Hardin is a biologist who believes that the competitive drive in humans is biologically mandated, that man must either struggle with other species or compete with his fellows. This view he derives from the old Malthusian notion that organisms tend to increase geometrically while the environmental support system is finite.[98]

Hardin believes altruism possible but only on a small scale, over the short run, in certain circumstances, and within small, intimate groups. When both altruists and egoists are thrown together in large, impersonal groups, enlightened egoism is the more powerful motive and any realistic society must therefore rely on it.[99] He urges that in scarcity conditions such as we today live under it is not superior morality that is most likely to serve posterity but an institutional design that makes use of special privilege. Distributive justice is a luxury that cannot be afforded by a country in which population overcomes the resource base. Carrying capacity, not lives, must be saved not only for posterity but even for this generation.[100]

Clearly Hardin's views rejecting utopian egalitarianism as unscientific are a direct link to the new social Darwinists, whose guru is the noted ethologist Konrad Lorenz. Lorenz provides the common denominator for the new social Darwinism in the claim that human beings are instinctively aggressive, just as are most higher vertebrates.[101] Lorenz poses the ineradicability of the human aggressive drive and proposes that the best way to mitigate its harmful impact is to restore the primate social hierarchy which the well-intentioned myth of human equality has sought to destroy. Present-day civilized man suffers from insufficient discharge of his aggressive drive.[102]

Robert Ardrey, a populizer of Lorenz, has written a series of books designed to prove that man is the direct descendant of a killer ape, which allegedly establishes a biological basis for the aggressive nature of man and the competitive societies he cherishes.[103] From this Ardrey derives the inevitability of a private-property system, capitalism, social hierarchy, authority wielders, and the instinct of territoriality in human groups, the so-called territorial imperative.[104] The "romantic fallacy" which aims at creating a society of equals is a natural impossibility,[105] a theme which Ardrey picks up from Lorenz.

The zoologist Desmond Morris also sees man as the descendant of a primate predator who has determined his fundamental behavior patterns; millions of years are still needed to change man's hunter mentality and concomitant social practice: hierarchical relations, intraspecific aggression, and assumption of a tribal identity.[106] This is essentially the same picture which emerges from the works of anthropologists Lionel Tiger and Robin Fox, for whom man is still the upper-Paleolithic hunter. They see societies in evolutionary terms as a breeding process in which the distribution of genes is the struggle for reproductive advantage, the result being a profoundly hierarchical and competitive social system.[107] Thus man, a naturally aggressive and acquisitive animal, is bent on the pursuit of status.[108]

The psychiatrist Anthony Storr adds that aggression in man is instinctive. The body contains a coordinated physico-chemical system which subserves the aggressive emotions and is easily triggered by the stimuli of threat and frustration.[109] To believe that there has been or can be an era of aggression-free perfect peace or a world without competition or aggression is unrealistic. Such a world would be stripped of the creative aspect of aggression and competition to which civilization owes its finest hours.[110]

It has been pointed out by critics of the Lorenz-Morris-Fox-Ardrey axis that their arguments are only as good as their analogy between animal and human behavior, and especially the inference involved in asserting that behavior is instinctive. These critics assert that there is no biological theory of genes which makes it possible to differentiate between instinctive mechanisms of behavior.[111] The sociobiologist David P. Barash considers it pointless to debate whether humans are innately aggressive, especially since genetic and environmental factors are, as he says, so intimately interrelated in the determination of such behavior.[112] The question emerges as to the scientific value of the concept of human instinct. Much of what Lorenz considers to be innate animal behavior has been criticized as vulgar oversimplification: he is accused of failure to discriminate between the different kinds of levels of behavior and the multiplicity of casual factors involved in each.[113] As one ethologist critic of Lorenz puts it, there is a long way from the genes to behavior.[114] And as to Lorenz's crucial hypothesis of the spontaneity of the aggression instinct in animals, the ethologist John Hurrell Crook counters that there is in fact no uncontroversial evidence that in the absence of stimulation, aggressiveness must find a spontaneous outlet.[115] Crook sees the manifestation of aggression in human society as largely a cultural attribute.[116] Crook's conclusions are suported by the data of the experimental psychologist John Paul Scott, who studied the physiology of animal aggression and concluded that there is a complex network of causal stimuli, no one of which entirely accounts for aggressive behavior. The chain of causation always is traced eventually to the outside: there is no physiological evidence of any innate spontaneous stimulation for fighting among animals.[117] Traits are modified and limited by hereditary factors, but no trait, says Scott, is itself inherited.[118]

The eminent anthropologist Ashly Montagu does not deny that specific behavior in humans may be determined genetically, but stresses that while potentiality must be genetic in origin, particular abilities are learned.[119] Montagu concludes on the basis of post-Darwinian research that Darwin overemphasized in his theory of natural selection the role of competition and failed to recognize the importance of cooperation in evolution, which Montagu holds to be the biologically more dominant drive. His basis for this is his view of the fundamental fact that the reproductive act is the primary cooperative action.[120] Out of it we derive social life, dependency, and interdependency. The physiological dependency of the fetus and the newborn becomes, in society, a socially organized dependency in which the interacting persons finds the meaning of their lives in their mutual relations. Society is based on love. Aggression is a response to the denial of love. The organism is born with an innate need for love, with a need to respond to love, to be good, to be cooperative. And cooperative behavior has great survival value. Combativeness and competitiveness arise primarily from the frustration of the need to cooperate, hence they are secondary. Montagu, like Kropotkin, urges that our society substitute goodness for economics, that is, that self and society be regarded as intertwined. Man is for Montagu, who invokes the writings of Kropotkin, a good animal, and the evil surrounding him arises out of social arrangements, not the genes.[121]

The new branch of zoology, sociobiology, asserts that beneath the superficial aspects of social behavior exhibited by diverse animals lie common behavioral patterns governed by the genes and shaped by Darwinian evolution. Sociobiologists entertain the hypothesis that man's behavior may be as much a product of evolution as the structure of the hand or the size of the brain. Certain sociobiologists believe that human altruism is genetically transmitted and triggered whenever environmental circumstances are conducive. One of the foremost proponents of such views is Edward O. Wilson, a distinguished Harvard zoologist. Wilson allows that the intensity and forms of altruistic acts are largely culturally determined. What he considers to have evolved genetically is the underlying emotion. What the genes prescribe is not necessarily a particular behavior but the capacity to develop certain behaviors and the tendency to develop them in various specified environments.[122]

Like the Lorenzians, sociobiologists must assume the scientific nature of proposing analogies or homologies between the animal world and human society. Critics of sociobiology accuse it of being yet another variant of the recurrent determinist theories tending to provide a genetic justification for the social, economic, and political status quo.[123] One critic essentially equates Wilson with Ardrey by concluding that sociobiology's critical conclusion is that social behavior, including sexual division of labor, aggression, territoriality, and altruism as well as the very basis of our competitive capitalist system, are largely determined by genes and evolutions.[124] If there is a grave theoretical fallacy in biological determinism and a sinister ideological purpose hidden in its scientific baggage, the radical environmentalism which characterizes a sociobiological approach seems to carry a second social danger: assuming infinitely modifiable behavior must also assume that there are no real human needs or conditions. Freedom or creativity is no more required by human nature than their opposites, and we are faced with a value void.[125]

Kropotkin does not fall into either extreme. Drawing on both the genetic and environmentalist arguments, Kropotkin comes

closest to the position of cultural anthropologists like Ashley
Montagu and Alexander Alland, Jr.: that the cultural transmission
of social behavior does not preclude the existence of a genetic
component in all human behavioral traits, although the former is
the crucial mechanism in shaping human behavior.[126] For
Kropotkin the formation of a scientific ethics was premised on
the belief that altruism is indeed a stronger force than egoism
because of its greater species survival power, but Kropotkin
made it abundantly clear that only through the vigorous
inculcation of a cooperative ethics through society's cultural
transmission-belts would this superior force prevail. Kropotkin
emerges in terms of today's debate as a strong rather than a
radical environmentalist.

CHAPTER 5

The Living Intellectual Legacy of Kropotkin

G USTAV Landauer (1870-1919) was an original anarchist thinker whose translations of both Proudhon and Kropotkin brought their ideas into the German libertarian tradition. He attempted a synthesis of their ideas with his own the results of which clearly put him outside Kropotkinism. In 1904 both *Fields, Factories and Workshops* and *Mutual Aid* were translated, followed by *The Great French Revolution* in 1909. And while Landauer had translated Kropotkin as early as 1895, his own anarchist beliefs were well defined by the time he encountered Kropotkin's work.[1] Landauer insisted that Kropotkin's *Mutual Aid* and cooperation were not natural laws that operate in human life but rather desiderata of the human will.[2] For the better part of 1901, Landauer and Kropotkin were neighbors in England but were separated by Landauer's ignorance of France and Russia and his aversion to Kropotkin's communism. Kropotkin felt that Landauer was too much influenced by the individualism of Nietzsche and Ibsen.[3] Yet when Landauer wrote his major work, *Die Revolution*, in 1906-07, it was substantially influenced by *Mutual Aid* and its demonstration of the powerful European historical current of the voluntary cooperation of people and especially the medieval golden age of free cities and guilds.[4] While he drew upon Proudhon to argue for mutual credit as a basis for a rural mutualist, exchange economy of small farmers, artisans, and handicraftsmen, he drew upon Kropotkin's *Fields, Factories, and Workshops* for the sketch of his ideal small community, characterized by integrated work combining the physical and mental. Yet his emphasis was on spiritual regeneration as the chief virtue of the integrated community, not the Kropotkian emphasis on productivity. Moreover, Landauer saw

145

the state as a condition rather than a thing, as his disciple Martin Buber indicates. Therefore the real anarchist social order had to begin before any revolution. Thus, unlike Kropotkin, he renounced and even denounced class warfare or any form of proletarian party as futile. Such a party's task could only begin when the majority of the masses had joined it. Until then anarchist groups must only indulge in propaganda and composure. His advice to the proletariat was to withdraw from the capitalist system by forming work and consumer cooperatives.[6] Essentially then Landauer breaks entirely with the notion of the working class as the historically determined agent of social revolution. In fact for him the workers become increasingly dehumanized and thereby unrevolutionary as industrialization progresses.[7] Hence, his opposition to industrialization is far more inevitable. In sum, he is not a materialist or any other variant of a scientific revolutionary.

I *Kropotkin's Anarchist Progeny: Goldman and Berkman*

Emma Goldman (1869-1940), leading activist in the United States and in Spain during the Civil War, offered the anarchism of Kropotkin largely untouched. As her biographer Richard Drinnon is quick to admit, she was no theoretician. Perhaps, he suggests, her insistence that anarchism goes beyond economic change to every phase of life, added an aesthetic dimension to Kropotkin's thought and made her thinking of immediate relevance to contemporary cultural revolutionists.[8] She certainly added women's rights to the anarchist agenda. She was perhaps more emphatic than Kropotkin on the openness of the anarchist future:

> Because I believe that Anarchism can not consistently impose an iron-clad program or method on the future. The things every new generation has to fight, and which it can least overcome, are the burdens of the past, which hold us all as in a net. Anarchism, at least as I understand it, leaves posterity free to develop its own particular systems, in harmony with its needs.[9]

Like Kropotkin she insisted that there was no conflict between the individual and the social instincts, that the individual was the heart of society, conserving its essence.[10] Like Kropotkin, too, she stressed that labor productivity had already achieved the

ability to produce far beyond normal demands.[11] She generalized
on "propaganda by the deed," using the term "direct action." For
her this meant the open defiance of all laws and instructions.
Direct action was the logical, consistent method of anarchism.[12]

In one sense Goldman diverges from Kropotkin. She exchanges
his romanticism of the creative masses for a romanticism of the
heroic few. She sees herself as challenging the socialist
canonization of the majority, who represent the inertia and
tyranny of public opinion. The vital truth will out, in every
historical period, through the courage, individuality, free
initiative of enlightened minorities, the banner bearers.[13]

Alexander Berkman, also Russian born, joined Goldman in the
leadership of the American anarchist movement. His writings
were also substantially derivative from those of Kropotkin. Paul
Avrich considers his primer on anarchism, published in 1929, a
classic, ranking with Kropotkin's *Conquest of Bread* as the
clearest exposition of communist anarchism in any language.[14] In
it Berkman is far more emphatic than Kropotkin on the necessity
of constant class warfare. For him capital and government will
use any and all means to keep the proletariat in subjection: there
is an unremitting life-and-death struggle between capital and
labor.[15] Berkman is shrill and pointed where Kropotkin is calm
and didactic. He is out to taunt Americans for their smug myopia
about their much-vaunted democracy. Democracy is simply a
more clever game for the elite to play. He argues:

> That is why the average working man in the United States, though he
> has no more to say about the running of his country than the starved
> peasant in Russia had under the Tzar ... thinks he is free, while in fact
> he is only a wage slave.[16]

Like Kropotkin, Berkman insists on communist distribution
according to need because there is no way an individual's work
can be valued. The "lazy" and "inefficient" are casualties of the
capitalist division of labor for the need of useful activity is one of
the strongest of human instincts. At one point Berkman
challenges the need for an eight-hour work day in Kropotkin's
ringing tones and round figures:

> It can be statistically proven that three hours work a day at most, is
> sufficient to feed, shelter, and clothe the world and supply it not only
> with necessities but also with all modern comforts of life. The point is

that not one man in five is today doing any productive work. The entire world is supported by a small minority of toilers.[17]

Berkman's views on the revolutionary process also recall Kropotkin: a social revolution must uproot the foundations of society and must express a fundamental revision of ideas and opinions. It follows that the anarchist task is to shed light on present social evils and convince the masses of the practicability of anarchist values and vision. The revolution must be prepared in the sense of furthering the evolutionary process.[18] Berkman insists that anarchists do believe in organization, that the whole of life is organization, conscious or unconscious. But a good organization is a voluntary one of free and equal members.[19] While Kropotkin would hardly praise organization as crucial to anarchist strategy, the seemingly "new realism" of Berkman turns out to be an illusory departure since his organizational strength is utterly dependent upon voluntary individual coopera-tion.

Berkman fleshes out somewhat more than Kropotkin the mechanism of direct, moneyless exchange under anarchist-communism.[20] But like his mentor, Berkman sees the market categories of exchange value and money as universal equivalent in contradiction with a communist economy. Again like Kro-potkin, his insight need not be faulted but rather his failure theoretically to sustain it. Berkman makes no attempt to come to grips with the problem of transition, the complexity of determin-ing priorities, the societal costs of foregoing alternative uses, and the necessity of determining a system of measurement compati-ble with communist economic and political relations in order to compare the social utilities of products.

II   Kropotkinism Transformed: Herbert Read and the Nonrevolutionary Road

Probably the most impressive anarchist writer of the 1930s and 1940s was Herbert Read, the British art critic and historian. Read preached that the Spanish Civil War proved conclusively that anarcho-syndicalism could work, and he provided a sketch of the future to show us how:

Each industry forms itself into a federation of self-governing collectives; the control of each industry is wholly in the hands of the workers in that industry, and these collectives administer the whole economic life of the country. That there will be something in the nature of a parliament of industry to adjust mutual relations between various collectives and to decide on general questions of policy goes without saying, but this parliament will be in no sense an administrative or executive body. It will form a kind of industrial diplomatic source, adjusting relations and preserving peace, but possessing no legislative powers and no privileged status. There might also be a corresponding body to represent the interests of the consumers, and to arrange questions of price and distribution with the collectives.[21]

Read challenges those who attack the allegedly utopian dream of anarchism by proclaiming that the task of the anarchist philosopher is not to prove the imminence of a Golden Age, but to justify the value of believing in its possibility. For Read, passionate, unstructured, and spontaneous rebellion may, if successful, leave in its wake a transformed human nature and a new morality. This change would imply the renunciation of power in human relations:

Unless a society can renounce power, and the deliberate actions which arise from the desire to exercise power, there is no escape from the "insanity of history." A power structure is the form taken by the inhibition of creativity: the exercise of power is the denial of spontaneity. The will to power, an emotional complex in individuals, directly conflicts with the will to mutuality, which, as Kropotkin showed, is a social instinct. The will to power is an eccentric and disruptive force: the unity it would impose is totalitarian. Mutuality is unity itself, and is creative. When men rebel against tyranny, they are affirming, not their individuality but the unity of their human nature; they are affirming their desire to create a unity on the basis of their common ideals (of truth or beauty).[22]

Read holds Bakunin's legacy to be a heroic one but with no practical message for the present age. Kropotkin, equally heroic, was more practical but his plans too have been overtaken by the intensive development of modern methods of production. Syndicalism is now the only practical form of anarchism, with the local unit of government in control of all immediate interests and elective councils dealing with questions of cooperation and foreign affairs. If we can make politics local, we can make them real. . . .[23] Read adds that delegates should be *ad hoc,* the profession of politician abolished, and representation based on a functional basis. The proof of this political pudding, he feels, is the medieval commune.[24]

Mutual aid will be the foundation of the anarchist social order,[25] and the very Kropotkinian measure of social efficiency will be "appetite for fullness of living."[26]

Read raises the Kropotkinian banner of biology over the Marxian banner of economics, claiming anarchism is based on the former and Marxism on the latter. Anarchism does not deny the importance of economic forces and class struggle but it insists that consciousness of an overridding human solidarity is the more important factor.[27] The aggressive instinct, which is the basis of the will to power, can be transformed into creative channels and become the very essence of mutual love, of communism. In sum, Read finds Kropotkin's conclusions in *Mutual Aid* strictly scientific.[28]

III   *Kropotkinism in Contemporary Anarchist Terms: Murray Bookchin and Colin Ward*

The leading anarchist-communist in America today, Murray Bookchin, is a creative thinker and critic who infuses his critique of present-day capitalism and Marxism with Kropotkinian visions of a new, free, decentralized society. For Bookchin, like Kropotkin, the present is a postscarcity society and the foremost contradiction of capitalism is the tension between the actuality of domination and the potentiality of freedom. Nor does this contradiction disappear according to Bookchin, with the advent of state socialism:

Hierarchy, sexism and renunciation do not disappear with "democratic centralism," a "revolutionary leadership," a "workers' state," and a "planned economy." On the contrary, hierarchy, sexism and renunciation function all the more effectively if centralism appears to be "democratic," if leaders appear to be "revolutionaries," if the state appears to belong to the 'workers' and if the commodity production appears to be "planned." Insofar as the socialist project fails to note the very existence of these elements, much less their vicious role, the "revolution" itself becomes a facade for counter-revolution. Marx's vision notwithstanding, what tends to "wither away" after this kind of revolution is not the state but the very consciousness of domination.[29]

Bookchin rebukes Marxism and socialism in general for subverting the ideal of liberation from toil and replacing it with the work ethic. He, like Kropotkin, sees the potential for technological development providing machine substitutes for human labor as virtually unlimited.[30] The perverse, inhuman fragmentation of jobs into their mini-components effected by capitalism and state socialism in the name of cost efficiency, projects, and growth, can be reversed by the same technology that abetted this dehumanization. Miniaturized electronic components, smaller production facilities and highly versatile, multipurpose machines can make practical small or moderate-sized communities, striking a "humanistic balance ... between autarky, industrial confederation, and a national division of labor."[31]

For Bookchin, the emphasis on "direct action" as a basic revolutionary strategy is more than a tactical tool. It is a mode of praxis intended to promote the individuation of the masses. Its psychological effect is to make practitioners aware of themselves as individuals who can affect their own destiny. Anarchist praxis emphasizes spontaneity, a conception of praxis as an inner process, not external manipulation. This process does not fetishize undifferentiated impulse but evokes a multi-level feeling permeated by knowledge, insight, and experience. Belief in spontaneity is part of the larger belief in spontaneous development. For Bookchin every development must be free to find its own equilibrium. Spontaneity is not chaos. Rather it releases inner forces of development in search of authentic order and stability.[32]

Bookchin says that the ecological movement has tended to a rediscovery of the importance of spontaneity. It has shown that the balance in nature is achieved by organic variation and complexity, not by homogeneity and simplification. Man can improve ecological quality by insight and understanding, not the exercise of brute force and manipulation. Capitalist agriculture organized as a factory operation of immense scale, specialization, centralization, chemicalization, and mechanization is challenged. Bookchin hopes to create a new sensitivity to ecological needs and to the need for a humanly scaled and diversified environment. Moreover, only by developing small industrial units with diversified energy sources can pollution be alleviated. The technology is at hand. Miniaturized substitutes for factory complexes using a single energy source have already been developed: small, versatile machines and sophisticated methods for converting solar, wind, and water energy into power usable in industry and at home.[33]

Bookchin labels the saturation of the soils with nitrate, insecticides, herbicides, and other toxic compounds a new type of pollution, soil pollution. He opposes radical agriculture to the prevailing technicist and instrumentalist approach which equates cultivation with an assault on nature: a capitalist legacy incompatible with any sense of community, whether with nature or in society.

Variety in both society and agriculture, Bookchin urges, must be promoted as a positive value. The more complex the food webs, the more stable the biotic structure. For Bookchin, the most disastrous aspect of prevailing agricultural methodologies, with their emphasis on monoculture, crop hybrids, and chemicals, has been the simplification they have introduced into food cultivation globally. A truly ecological viewpoint is not just interested in managing nature with a minimum of pollution but rather in seeing the biotic world as a holistic unity—a community of which humanity is a part. Radical agriculture is more than new techniques in food cultivation: it is a "promethean sensibility toward land and society as a whole."[34]

The sociopolitical implications for Bookchin are that the basic communal unit of social life must become an eco-system, an eco-community, diversified, balanced, and well-rounded. Its individual analogue is the well-rounded man, and the liberation of daily life from monotony and hardship.[35] The anarchist concepts of a balanced community, a face-to-face democracy, a humanistic technology, and a decentralized society are not only desirable but absolutely necessary. They constitute the preconditions for human survival. They are eminently practical.[36]

On the perennial problem of anarchism and organization, Bookchin says the question is not whether there must be an organization but rather what kind. Anarchist-communism cannot deny the need for coordination between groups, for discipline, planning, and unity in action. But these must be achieved voluntarily, nourished by conviction and understanding rather than coercion. The task of the revolutionary organization is not administration but propaganda. And in a revolutionary situation, it must formulate the tactics that will advance the revolutionary process.[37] While closer than Kropotkin to granting the necessity of an anarchist party, Bookchin stops far short of explaining how individual praxes are to be effectively coordinated.

The English anarchist Colin Ward has been associated with the reissuance of Kropotkin's *Fields, Factories and Workshops.* He was an editor of the British anarchist weekly *Freedom* from 1947 to 1960 and also helped edit the monthly *Anarchy* from 1961 to 1970. These publications are the living heirs of Kropotkin's English anarchist organization. Ward insists on the practicality of workers' control in technologically complex societies. The obstacles are not technical or economic but the vested interests of the privileged.

In embryonic forms, syndicalism has already offered an example of production control by direct producers. For a lump sum, allocated among its members as it saw fit, a syndicalist work group contracted for a specific output on condition that management cede control over the production process. Ward also refers to the noted student of managerial economics Seymour Melman, whose *Decision Making and Productivity* sought to demonstrate that the workers' collective is a realistic alternative to managerial diktat. Melman not only concluded that the group voice of a collective has the greater motivational impact but contrasted its "mutuality" with the predatory competition of the managerial decision-making process.[38] Ward emphasizes that such "encroaching control" at the workplace can point to a new anarchist strategy: the pitfalls of premature revolutionary action and nonrevolutionary reformism can be avoided.

Ward argues, as do Bookchin and Kropotkin, that changes in the sources of motive power make the geographical concentration of industry obsolete, as automation outdates the concentration of vast numbers of workers. Decentralization is perfectly feasible and probably economically advantageous even within the confines of contemporary technology.[39]

In light of the fact that many consumer-oriented industries are substantially involved in assembling components made elsewhere, Ward urges a return to old fashion domestic industry:

Groups of community workshops could combine for bulk ordering of components, or for sharing according to their capacity the production of components for mutual exchange and for local assembly.[40]

An anarchist society would produce objects whose functioning would be transparent and whose repair could be readily undertaken by the user.[41] Thus, parasitic repair and service sectors ancillary to the production function could be minimized and substantially localized.

Ward believes that Kropotkin's vision of decentralized industry under the control of local producers and consumers, who alternate brainwork and manual labor, is being realized in China today.[42] He feels that the Chinese experiment demonstrates not only that technology can serve need instead of profit but that political reorientation can lead to reorganization of the production forces—indeed the redefinition of political economy:

> Size and resources are to the technologist what power is to the politician; he can never have too much of them. A different kind of society, with different priorities, would evolve a different technology: its bases already exist and in terms of the tasks to be performed it would be far more "efficient" than either Western capitalism or Soviet state-capitalism. Not only technology but also economics would have to be redefined. Per Kropotkin, political economy tends to become a science devoted to the study of the needs of men and of the means of satisfying them with the least possible waste of energy.[43]

IV   Kropotkinist Ideas and Neo-Anarchism: Carter and Mumford

April Carter believes that anarchism has acquired more, rather than less, relevance today. Anarchist ideas, she feels, may be important in the reinterpretation of liberalism and socialism and may be partially realized in the aims of popular movements.[44] Kropotkin's ideas on decentralization of industry have substantially affected Lewis Mumford, surely one of the most perceptive critics of industrial society in this century. In his two-volume study, *The Myth of the Machine*, Mumford explores our age as one of transition from the progressive mastery of nature through the invention of tools and weapons to a radically different condition in which man has detached himself as far as possible from the organic habitat. Speculates Mumford:

> With this new "megatechnics" the dominant minority will create a uniform, all enveloping, super-planetary structure, designed for automatic operation. Instead of functioning actively as an autonomous

personality, man will become a passive, purposeless, machine-conditioned animal whose proper functions, as technicians now interpret man's role, will either be fed into the machine or strictly limited and controlled for the benefit of de-personalized, collective organizations.[45]

Mumford's purpose, in his own words, "is to question both the assumptions and the predictions upon which our commitment to the present forms of technical and scientific progress, treated as if ends in themselves, has been based." Mumford holds that our predecessors mistakenly coupled their particular mode of mechanical progress with an unjustifiable sense of increasing moral superiority. Our own contemporaries have reason to reject this smug Victorian belief in the inevitable improvement of all human institutions through command of the machine. Yet they concentrate with "manic fervor" upon the continued expansion of science and technology as if they would magically provide the only means of human salvation. Mumford believes our present overcommitment to technics is in part due to a radical misinterpretation of the whole course of human development: namely, that man is essentially a tool-making animal.[46]

Mumford places central emphasis on man's overdeveloped and incessantly active brain, which provides more mental energy than he needs for survival. Only by creating cultural outlets can man fully utilize and control his own nature.[47] The dominant human trait for Mumford is the capacity for conscious, purposeful self-identification, self-transformation, and self-understanding.[48]

Mumford stresses the primacy of art through the ages as a stimulant to technics and a quintessential expression of the human need to confer significance on the external world through the creating of symbolic systems. Our power-worshiping society judges art and handicrafts backward by its provincial standards of machine worship, love of mass-consumption, and disregard for individuality, variety, and choice. Yet until the rise of European capitalism the most intense human energies have always poured into the arts of expression and communication. Until the machine monopolized our attention, there was a continual interplay between quantitative order and working efficiency on the one hand, and the qualitative values and purposes that reflected the human personality on the other. And the reciprocal relation between art and technics was maintained to their common advantage through all the ages of small-scale handicraft production. It was in the decorative, the symbolic, and the expressive arts that progress was maintained, even in ages which from our technicist perspective have seemed stagnant. Mumford feels that this contribution has been underrated, even in its technical implications. After the sixteenth century the craft-technical tradition was progressively destroyed by the "invention of invention," which gave to the machine the primacy that had once belonged to the craftsman-artist, and which reduced the personality to just those numbered parts that could be transferred to the machine.[49]

Ironically but tragically, comments Mumford, this process climaxed just when democratic technics, centered in the small workshop, had at last at its command sufficient mechanical power to rival the megamachine:

With the introduction of small-scale power machinery, which could have increased quantitative production without destroying aesthetic sensibility or undermining personal creativity, the flowering of the arts that took place in Europe from the thirteenth century on might have gone on steadily. A genuine polytechnics was in the making, capable of reconciling the order and efficiency of the megamachine with the creative initiative and individuality of the artist. But within a few centuries the whole system was undermined by the new impersonal market economy and the resurrection in a new form of the totalitarian megamachine.[50]

While the pool of complex and technically superior machines has enormously increased over the last century, the technological pool has actually been dried up as surviving handicrafts dwindle. The result is that monotechnics, based upon scientific intelligence and quantitative production, directed mainly toward economic expansion, material depletion, and military superiority, has superseded polytechnics, based primarily, as in agriculture, on the needs, aptitude, and interests of living organisms. Both the tool and the tool user have almost disappeared. Today what cannot be done by a power machine or replaced by the factory must be scrapped.[51]

Yet there was no reason to make a wholesale choice between handicraft and machine production. Rather there was a genuine reason to maintain as many diverse units in the technological pool as possible. Many of the machines of the nineteenth century were admirable auxiliaries to handicraft processes, once they could be scaled, like the small, efficient electric motor, to the workshop and the personally controlled operation.[52]

Mumford cites two thinkers of the last century, Peter Kropotkin and Patrick Geddes, as especially quick to realize advantages of an advanced technology for restoring humanly scaled production and with it the mutuality of a face-to-face community without forfeiting the benefits of rapid communication and transportation. Kropotkin is singled out for having grasped that the flexibility and adaptability of electric communication and power along with intensive biodynamic farming could lay the foundation for decentralized urban development and break down the urban-rural divide. Most important, he placed a social order based on plenitude on the historical agenda. Mumford finds it curious that, without being conscious of any prior analysis, Dr. Norbert Wiener, whose own scientific work furthered automation, rediscovered the possibilities which Kropotkin had outlined two generations earlier in *Fields, Factories and Workshops*. For Mumford, Kropotkin must be included among the finest minds of the nineteenth century.[53]

V   Kropotkinist Ideas and Neo-Anarchism: Goodman, Merrill, Berry

The late Paul Goodman evokes the Kropotkinian spirit in his presentation of alternatives to our overly centralized, overly organized, and overly crowded urban-industrial society. Goodman, like Kropotkin, sees the system of voluntary association as most productive of cultural values and Goodman echoes Kropotkin in emphasizing the need to revive peasant self-reliance and the democratic power of professional and technical guilds and workers' councils: to find contemporary analogues for the independence, multifarious skills, communal and family ties that were valued in the small rural community.[54]

Goodman's portrait of today's large-scale, top-down organization is characterized by local initiative smothered and information distorted between the field and the center by insulating bureaucratic layers. In decentralized conditions, these distortions and inhibitions yield to the competent, emancipated individual. Goodman echoes Kropotkin and Mumford in questioning the value of our society's emphasis on mass production

and quantity: "A rational economist must finally be concerned
with how well people live, not what things cost. In measuring the
wealth of society, it is absurd to rely entirely on its Gross
National Product...."[55]

Goodman points out four areas where excessive centralization
is grossly expensive:

(1) where staff and overhead are the chief costs;
(2) where the costs of distribution or servicing outweigh the savings
    in centralized production;
(3) where centralized planning and rationalization go beyond the
    flowing changes and contingencies of life and lead to overcom-
    mitment and inflexibility;
(4) where the departmentalization and standardization, which miss
    the uniqueness of each person, produce imbalances and positive
    damage that must be expensively remedied.[56]

Goodman, like Kropotkin and Mumford, asserts that urbanization is not a technical necessity. Electricity, power tools, autos,
communication, and automation would seem to allow for
deurbanization, dispersal of population and industry. Nor is
urbanization a necessity of population growth. With the
bankruptcy of small farmers, vast and beautiful regions have
been depopulating. Yet the prevailing social and political
policies spawned by urbanization are careless of social and even
economic costs.[57] To relieve the growing avarice of our urban
wastelands, Goodman recommends experiments with new communal organization and with new forms of democracy. Population dispersal can be achieved through rural reconstruction and
the reconstitution of country towns or regional capitals rather
than more "New Towns" and satellite, dormitory suburbs.[58]

Like Kropotkin, Goodman sees small-scale agriculture playing
a vital role near urban centers not just to prevent suburbaniza-
tion but to supply essential foodstuffs:

With some crops, certainly with specialty and gourmet food, the
system of intensive cultivation and hothouses serving farmer markets in
the city and contracting with restaurants and hotels is quite efficient: it
omits processing and packaging, cuts down on the cost of transportation, and is indispensable for quality. The development of technology in
agricultures has no doubt been, as with technology in general, largely
determined by economic policy and administration. If there were a
premium on small intensive cultivation, as in Holland, technology would
develop to make it the "most efficient."[59]

Again, Kropotkin provides the inspiration for Goodman's insistence that genuine farmers' cooperatives, intensive organic farming, and small community self-sufficiency are intimately related to the prospects of rural revitalization and population dispersal through a policy of combining and balancing industry and agriculture.[60]

Kropotkin's precocious ecological concerns and his emphasis upon the perverse short-term rationality of overcentralization and specialization in industry and agriculture are concerns which are now being very much discussed and acted upon. It would seem no exaggeration to consider Kropotkin the forerunner of the new ecology and the godfather of modern organic farming.

Much of what Kropotkin could only guess would come to pass has indeed emerged in the agricultural area. There is a feeling today that the era of cheap, abundant food is over and that industrialized agriculture has been a short-term marvel with long-term costs to society. These include the loss of quality, the destruction of our rural culture and environment, the rise of centralized food monopolies, and the gigantic exodus from farm to city. Since 1948 over 25 million people in the United States have been relocated to urban centers—largely because of the rise of technologically intensive farming and agribusiness. As Richard Merrill observes, the abandonment of farmlands and the separation of people from their land and food resources have become symbols of our social progress. But it is by no means obvious that the depopulation of rural areas and the con-centralization of agriculture have produced a just, stable, and fulfilling society.[61] Like Bookchin, Merrill stresses the pollution and health problems caused by salt fertilizers, livestock chemi-cals, and pesticides. He concludes that there is growing evidence that higher yields will not warrant the costs of new tech-nologies—especially those, as in the American model, requiring high inputs of dwindling fossil fuels.[62]

As to the grim statistics on the Jeffersonian yeomanry, each year 100,000 farms are abandoned and over the last fifty years over 40 million people have left rural America.[63] Since 1940, the number of farms has been reduced from 6.3 million to 2.9 million, with 1 million gone since 1961. At the same time the farm population has been reduced from 31.9 million (23.2 percent of the population in 1940) to 9.7 million (4.8 percent of the population in 1970) though the total farm acreage remained around 1 billion acres.[64] More than 1.5 million of the remaining farmers are earning less than poverty-level farm incomes. Although the U.S. census counts 2.9 million farmers, 50,000 grow one-third of the country's food supply and 200,000 produce more than half of all food.

Why is this? Was Kropotkin's faith misplaced not only in a trend away from large-scale industry and agriculture but also in the economic competitiveness of the smaller production units? Does the centralization of agriculture indicate the inherent virtues of larger-scale production? Peter Barnes observes that large farms in America are efficient at tapping the federal treasury and exploiting hired labor. If you take away these privileges, he feels, the small farmer looks extremely good.[65] Barnes points out that an increasing number of Americans are not really free to assume responsibilities or to make major decisions affecting their lives, since they either work for large corporations or government bureaucracies or on assembly lines. He urges that revitalization of small-scale farming could be a remedy. Michael Perelman also sees the profitability of large-scale agriculture as a political bequest largely due to tax "write-offs," privileged treatment of capital gains, and the farm subsidy system. The economic rationale for large-scale farming is not production efficiency but marketplace leverage, which is rewarded by cheaper inputs and better and cheaper access to bank loans.[66]

Wendell Berry questions the contemporary use of the economic concept of efficiency. He feels it means cheapness at any price, the profligate waste of humanity and nature, and the greatest profit to the greatest liar:

What we have called efficiency has produced among us, and to our incalculable cost, such unprecedented monuments of destructiveness and waste as the strip-mining industry, the Pentagon, the federal bureaucracy, and, to some, the family car.

Real efficiency is something entirely different. It is neither cheap (in terms of skill and labor) nor fast. Real efficiency is long-term efficiency. It is to be found in means that are in keeping with the preserving of their ends, in methods of production that preserve the sources of production, in workmanship that is durable and of high quality. In this age of consumerism, planned obsolescence, frivolous horsepower, and surplus manpower, those salesmen and politicians who talk about efficiency are talking, in reality, about spiritual and biological death.[67]

Specialization for hire has become a destructive force. It has increased knowledge but fragmented it as well: the specialist no longer sees the effects of his discovery upon society. This is especially true in agriculture, where specialists have tended to think and work in terms of piecemeal solutions and annual production, rather than in terms of a coherent system that would maintain the fertility and the ecological health of the land over a period of centuries. Like Bookchin and Kropotkin, Berry insists that a healthy agriculture—indeed a healthy biotic system—is diversified, and that long-term agricultural productivity requires a stable rural community bound in sympathy and association to the land. He ends on the Kropotkinian note that farming is not a technique or laboratory science but praxis, an art which grows out of cultural tradition.[68]

VI *Kropotkinist Ideas and Neo-Anarchism: McLeod, Comfort, Schumacher.*

Darryl McLeod recalls Kropotkin in advocating municipal economic sovereignty as the way to the new agriculture:

The recurrent crop shortages, transportation problems, and absurdly high raw produce prices of recent years cast doubt on the wisdom of regional crop specialization, long distance shipping of foodstuff, and the very industrial foundations of the modern food industry. Placed in the midst of these monocultures and huge food factories and supermarketing wonders, small diversified farms would be an aberration. But in the context of the preordering networks that are beginning to develop, such urban-fringe farms are not only desirable but necessary.... [The] rural, ecological, and social ramifications (of a polyculture farm) dovetail nicely with the aspirations and efforts of today's urban neighborhoods. Urban food organizing has been able to provide the new experimental "organic" farms with more than a dependable, predictable year-round outlet for its variety of produce.[69]

Alex Comfort is a far-ranging cultural critic whose vision of socioeconomic problems, human sexuality, and sociology evince a clear anarchist influence. Like Marcuse, Comfort is interested in the effects of repressive social systems on the human psyche. Like Kropotkin, Comfort sees meaningful work as a socializing force, equal to art and religion, which can discharge both aggression and constructive drives in a single act.[70]

Comfort sees the impulse to constructive labor and to sociality as the "natural" inputs into social organization. Recalling Kropotkin, he states: "The impulse of sociality, distorted by many forms of unreason and moulded by stress into many destructive . . . patterns, is still the most clearly discernible thread in human cultures."[71] It is not surprising that Comfort considers Kropotkin's theory of mutual aid of immense biological and social relevance. Kropotkin is hailed as the first systematic student of animal communities and the founder of modern social ecology. Comfort sees penology today much as Kropotkin did, inefficacious in statistical terms, and used essentially as a cheap substitute for the reconstruction of society.[72]

For Comfort, repression has been the historical product of the use of government to express two incompatible social activities: organization or communication and individual or group dominance. He urges that we cease to regard government as a matter of power and begin to regard it as a matter of communication,[73] and that the mechanics of democratic expression are a straight— and solvable—problem in communication theory![74] The new society would be nourished by the full potential of our technological pool along with the communal and symbolic values of preindustrial cultures. Cohesion and order would be maintained by the psychology of individuals, not by any system of institutional powers as we know them. The mutuality of fear would be replaced by the exchange of personal responsibility— by mutual aid.[75]

The late E. F. Schumacher wrote an influential critique of conventional economics entitled *Small Is Beautiful—Economics As If People Mattered.* The introduction to this work, by Theodore Roszak, places Schumacher's book in the subterranean tradition of organic and decentralist economics whose major spokesmen include Kropotkin, Gustav Landauer, Tolstoi, William Morris, Gandhi, Mumford, and, most recently, Alex Comfort, Paul Goodman, and Murray Bookchin. For Roszak, this underground community can be defined by its insistence that the scale of organization must be treated as an independent and primary problem.[76]

Schumacher's starting point is his alarm at the startling rate at which Western capitalism is using up natural capital. Allied to the quantum jump in the increasing rate of industrial consumption since 1945 is the unprecedented problem of nature's inability to absorb or break down the new chemical compounds thrust upon her. Schumacher labels the illusion that the problem of production has been solved one of the most fateful errors of our age, based as it is on the failure to recognize that the modern industrial system consumes the very foundations on which it has been erected: fossil fuel, the tolerance margins of nature, and the human substance. Schumacher urges that for human survival we had better begin to see the possibility of evolving a new life-style with new methods of production and new patterns of consumption, designed for permanence. Industry must evolve small-scale technology based on the family and work group; social experiment must lead to new forms of partnership between management and workers, new forms of common ownership.[77]

The attitude of the singleminded pursuit of wealth cannot fit into the necessary new world because it contains within itself no limiting principle, whereas the support system it depends on and abuses is strictly limited. From an economic point of view, Schumacher insists that the central concept of wisdom is permanence.[78] The cultivation and expansion of needs is the antithesis of wisdom, freedom, and peace. Every increase in needs tends to increase one's dependence on outside forces beyond one's control. Only by reducing needs and the tension they generate can we undermine or mitigate the causes of strife and war.

Wisdom demands a new orientation of science and technology toward the organic, the gentle, the elegant, and the beautiful. What is needed are methods and equipment which are cheap enough so that they are accessible to virtually everyone and suitable for small-scale application as well as compatible with man's need for creativity. Small-scale operations, no matter how numerous, are far less likely to be harmful to the natural environment than mass production, because individual force is small in relation to the recuperative forces of nature. Moreover, adds Schumacher, there is wisdom in smallness if only because we rely far more on empirical experiment than on rational understanding and must have the modesty to avoid consequences of large-scale application of partial knowledge.[79]

Schumacher condemns soul-destroying, meaningless, mechanical, monotonous, moronic work as an insult to human nature which necessarily produces either escapism or aggression, which no amount of "bread and circuses" can neutralize or compensate.[80] And these debasements are justified in the name of economics: whether they yield a money profit to those who initiate them. Profit or loss to society is left out of the calculations, not only in the sense of short-term externalities but in terms of a legacy to future generations. Schumacher notes that it is inherent in the methodology of economics to ignore man's dependence on the natural world.[81] In the market everything has a price and nothing is sacred. Noneconomic values like beauty, health, and cleanliness can survive only if they pass a cost-benefit analysis in dollars and cents.[82] Vital distinctions between primary and secondary goods, and within the primary, between renewable and nonrenewable, are ignored.[83]

Modern technology, unlike nature, recognizes no self-limiting principle. It is not a feedback mechanism that can self-balance, self-adjust, self-cleanse.[84] The poor of the world cannot be helped by capital-intensive mass production which displaces human labor and depends on costly energy-inputs and imports. This is a technology only for the rich: inherently violent, ecologically damaging, and self-defeating in terms of non-renewable resources, and stultifying for the human being through the social and technical division of labor it implies.

Schumacher urges utilizing technology on a human scale in a decentralized setting compatible with ecology, gentle in its use of scarce resources, and designed to serve the operator's human needs. This he calls "intermediate technology";[85] it corresponds in substance to Kropotkin's miniaturization of machinery and implies the Kropotkinian principles of local self-sufficiency and rural reconstruction.

Unlike Kropotkin, Schumacher is not against private property as inherently unjust. Rather he sees private ownership of small-scale enterprise as natural and fruitful, although in medium-scale enterprises, private ownership to a large extent is functionally unnecessary. With large-scale enterprise, private ownership is a fiction which enables functionless owners to live parasitically on the labor of others.[86] Schumacher envisages a system whereby all large-scale enterprise is run by workers under local governmental scrutiny, with 50 per cent of the control and the profits going to the public.[87] And Schumacher, certainly no anarchist, sees society's overall direction, its financial and technological-scientific knowledge, as forming the context within which the local autonomy and national concerns are reconciled and interrelated.[88]

CHAPTER 6

Conclusions

K ROPOTKIN'S ideas were a living force in his time and remain so today. Many of his insights have stood the test of time remarkably well despite the failure of his views to cohere in a systematic construct. What is lacking in theoretical consistency and logical coherence as he freely analogizes from biology to history to economics is compensated by startling penetration into the implications of capitalist technological and industrial organization for the future of Western society and its physical environment.

As one of the first proponents of a humanly scaled technology and of coupling decentralization of industry with its dispersal to the countryside in search of balanced, wholesome communities, Kropotkin anticipated today's ecological, population-planning, and new-towns movements. In his endeavor to make agriculture on the urban fringe the basis of a realistic regional self-sufficiency, which would simultaneously thin out urban congestion and restore the economic viability of the rural hinterlands, he was a prophetic figure rather than a reactionary rural romantic. And his emphasis on organically intensive rather than technologically intensive agriculture joins a policy debate of the 1970s. In his attack upon Adam Smith's doctrine of the international and regional division of labor and the rela-tive-benefit theory, he made points which radical critics of developmental economics have made only recently. Kropotkin's arguments for a thoroughgoing egalitarianism, economically and socially, and his strong view of the crucial role of education are well worth reading in light of the present IQ controversy. It is possible to argue the relevance of his agro-industrial combines, with their dual economic and political personality, to the Chinese commune; Kropotkin's insight that the "productive forces" of society must be restructured in order to democratize

165

control of the productive process must have relevance to some Chinese and Yugoslav experiments; regional self-sufficiency has long been Maoist policy as has the coordination of artisanal technique with machinism ("walking on two legs"). Kropotkin's high regard for skilled labor and handicrafts, his emphasis upon the organic community, have resonance among a broad, even bewildering, array of social movements and groups today.

Kropotkin's respect for the peasantry and its vocation are in marked contrast to the patronization or theoretical and practical neglect of which many Western Marxists have been guilty. He very early incorporated the peasantry and the agricultural question into the center of the revolutionary agenda. In fact his revolutionary scenario in which the role of the peasant looms large better describes the successful revolutions of this century than Marxist "orthodoxy."

Kropotkin's attempt to prove the scientific imperative of altruism among animals and man remains unconvincing. But as a substantial critique of the "inherently evil" school of human nature and as a refutation of social Darwinism it has proved to be in harmony with the present consensus in the social and natural sciences. Kropotkin's attempt to base human ethics in biology may seem a misguided venture; but his concern with ethics, especially the relationship of revolutionary means to revolutionary ends and the measure of cultural attainment in terms of human satisfaction rather than output, are relevant to our social dialogue today. Many Marxists and neo-Marxists who have grappled with the ugly ramifications of a mass production system and a relentlessly industrialized landscape can turn to Kropotkin for guidance and inspiration. Equally important, Kropotkin has much to say on the question of the practicality of democracy. He hypothesized the relationship between community size and/or workshop size, on the one hand, and the degree of democratization of social relations and the productive process on the other. The question and theory of workers' control was central to Kropotkin's thinking, and this is a question that will not easily be erased from the social agenda.

For Kropotkin the whole man and the authentic life merged in work, but he insisted on the necessity—indeed "blessedness"— of leisure. Kropotkin's views on the significance of art represented his refusal to insulate the aesthetic from the practical. If, as the Greeks and Elizabethans would have it, art and artisan are makers, so can all men consciously make their environment, their community, their history beautiful.

Kropotkin's approach to nature is to include man in it, not to set him apart or see nature as something to be used or overcome. Free from technicist mediation, man's relation to nature is spiritual and aesthetic; it originates in respect for his sole life-support system and for a source of endless intricacies and wonders. Man's living rhythms are akin to and informed by nature's. Essentially this is what Kropotkin means by the irrepressible spontaneity of life. This is not anthropomorphism but a vision of human life in its total context. Kropotkin's views of the sources and motives of human behavior could have benefited from development and revision by passage through the crucible of intellectual exchange. He had his blind spots: his animosity toward Marx, his incongruous Francophilia. As historian and sociologist, he is hardly immune from the teleology and messianism of his era. His historical writings are especially superficial with the exception of his masterpiece on the French Revolution. Indeed much of his work bears the imprint of a flawed first draft. He is almost always sketchy, especially in regard to his writings on revolution, on the transition to and problems confronting the future society.

Many of his predictions about the social and economic trends of his day proved wrong and seem, at least with twenty-twenty hindsight, monuments to wishful thinking. The obvious examples are his belief in a tendency toward decentralization of industrial production and in the growing role of democratic private associations in assuming functions traditionally performed by various levels of government. Yet Kropotkin's powerful indictment of capitalism remains: neither his refusal of an incrementalist approach in order to examine the premises of his society nor his rejection of its value system can be dismissed as utopian. It is true that Kropotkin failed to make anarchism into a formidable revolutionary movement, surely the most grave of his political sins of omission. But despite his organizational failures, which substantially crippled the movement, Kropotkin was quite capable of "practical" politics and was always insistent on concrete proposals. He supported the Allies in World War I in order to keep alive what he believed to be the more progressive historical forces in France and England. The point is not that he was perhaps wrong in his analysis, but that he did feel a stake for his cause in the war's outcome. Kropotkin was frequently drawn into dialogue over incremental changes in society. He entered the lists for penal reform and in condemnation of the Tsarist system of justice; urged bourgeois governments to adopt educational and agricultural reforms. And he was able to revise his views in order to incorporate the lessons of the syndicalist movement, which he had originally accused of trade-unionism.

None of this diluted revolutionary commitment. Kropotkin never played at armchair revolution or at spare-time philosopher-king. He conveyed to friends and foes alike a monumental sense of moral outrage that would not be stilled or suspended for tactical or personal advantages. He was incorruptible and steadfast—yet humanitarian rather than fanatical.

Kropotkin's unflagging service in the cause of man's humanity to man is no small part of his legacy to a particularly brutal century. It became a leitmotif from the early days of challenging social Darwinism to the very end when, enfeebled and politically isolated, he interceded with Lenin on behalf of Bolshevik hostages.

Kropotkin must be adjudged a multi-faceted genius and a moral force. He was a justly famous scientist with distinction in both geography and geology, a pioneer in the field of sociobiology, the author of what remains a classic history of the French Revolution, and a major contributor to the literature on penology. His *Memoirs*, written with distinction and grace and in a characteristically self-effacing manner, are indisputably a classic source on the spirit and life of the privileged in nineteenth–century Russia. His correspondence with his brother constitutes a unique glimpse of the intellectual adolescence of the major anarchist thinker of all time. His arguments in favor of a radical egalitarianism and against the Malthusian-Social-Darwinian axis are among the most trenchant ever made.

As a moral philosopher Kropotkin continues to present us with an invaluable critique of Western society and an indictment of Western man's rapacious attitude toward nature, his self-serving morals, his glib rationalization of the cruel as "practical" in the name of what is sanctimoniously proclaimed the most civilized of societies and social systems. There is validity in faulting Kropotkin for oversimplifying the complexities of moral problems, but he could never be legitimately accused of hypocrisy.

This too is no small matter in an age when public officials have scaled new heights of venality and self-righteousness. And for all those implicated in the industrial megathon of the twentieth century, the challenge of Kropotkin's alternative—penultimate dispersal of economic and political power—remains unanswered.

45. N. K. Lebedev, "P. A. Kropotkin," *op cit.*, p. 20.
46. George Woodcock and Ivan Avakumovic, *op. cit.*, p. 25.
47. N. K. Lebedev, "P.A. Kropotkin," *op. cit.*, p. 21.
48. Martin A. Miller, "The Formative Years of P. A. Kropotkin," *op. cit.*, p. 51.
49. *Ibid.*, pp. 64-65.
50. George Woodcock and Ivan Avakumovic, "The Anarchist Prince," *op. cit.*, p. 37.
51. Martin A. Miller, "The Formative Years of P. A. Kropotkin. . .," *op. cit.*, pp. 69-70.
52. George Woodcock and Ivan Avakumovic, "The Anarchist Prince," *op. cit.*, p. 37.
53. Martin A. Miller, "The Formative Years of P. A. Kropotkin. . .," *op. cit.*, p. 73.
54. George Woodcock and Ivan Avakumovic, "The Anarchist Prince," *op. cit.*, pp. 38-39.
55. Nicholas Walter (ed.), "Peter Kropotkin, Memoirs of a Revolutionist," *op. cit.*, p. 127.
56. I. Smilga, "Predislovie," in *Petr i Aleksandr Kropotkiny Perepiska* (Moscow-Leningrad, 1932), I, 16-17.
57. *Ibid.*, p. 20.
58. Nicolas Walter (ed.), "Peter Kropotkin, Memoirs of a Revolutionist," *op. cit.*, pp. 94-95.
59. N. K. Lebedev, "Molodye Gody P. A. Kropotkina," in *Petr i Aleksandr Kropotkiny Perepiska*, I, 30.
60. *Ibid.*, pp. 53, 55.
61. *Ibid.*, pp. 84-85, 93-94.
62. *Petr i Aleksandr Kropotkiny Perepiska*, II, 96.
63. *Ibid.*, pp. 114-15.
64. *Ibid.*, p. 116.
65. *Ibid.*, pp. 128-29.
66. *Ibid.*, p. 137.
67. *Ibid.*, p. 181.
68. *Ibid.*, p. 187.
69. *Ibid.*, p. 193.
70. *Ibid.*, pp. 154-55.
71. *Ibid.*, p. 213.
72. *Ibid.*, p. 222.
73. Nicholas Walter (ed.), "Peter Kropotkin, Memoirs of a Revolutionist," *op. cit.*, p. 140.
74. N. K. Lebedev, "P. A. Kropotkin," *op. cit.*, pp. 21-22.
75. George Woodcock and Ivan Avakumovic, "The Anarchist Prince," *op. cit.*, p. 46.
76. Martin A. Miller, "The Formative Years of P. A. Kropotkin, 1842-1876," *op. cit.*, pp. 116-17.

77. *Petr i Aleksandr Kropotkiny Perepiska*, I, 262–63.
78. *Ibid.*, pp. 268–69.
79. N.K. Lebedev, "P. A. Kropotkin," *op. cit.*, p. 22.
80. George Woodcock and Ivan Avakumovic, "The Anarchist Prince," *op. cit.*, pp. 51, 53.
81. N. K. Lebedev, "P. A. Kropotkin," *op. cit.*, p. 22.
82. *Petr i Aleksandr Kropotkiny Perepiska*, II, 38–39.
83. *Dnevnik P. A. Kropotkina* (Moscow-Petrograd, 1923), p. 7.
84. George Woodcock and Ivan Avakumovic, "The Anarchist Prince," *op. cit.*, p. 54.
85. "Dnevnik P. A. Kropotkina," *op. cit.*, p. 45.
86. *Petr i Aleksandr Kropotkiny Perepiska*, II, 44–45.
87. *Ibid.*, p. 49.
88. *Ibid.*, p. 54.
89. *Ibid.*, pp. 15–16.
90. *Ibid.*, pp. 15–16, 23.
91. Martin A. Miller, "The Formative Years of P. A. Kropotkin, 1842–1876," *op. cit.*, pp. 159–61.
92. *Petr i Aleksandr Kropotkiny Perepiska*, II, 79.
93. *Ibid.*, p. 73.
94. Martin A. Miller, "The Formative Years of P. A. Kropotkin, 1842–1876," *op. cit.*, pp. 187–88.
95. *Petr i Aleksandr Kropotkiny Perepiska*, II, 166.
96. Martin A. Miller, "The Formative Years of P. A. Kropotkin, 1842–1876," *op. cit.*, pp. 189–90.
97. *Peter i Aleksandr Kropotkiny Perepiska*, II, 123–24.
98. "P. A. Kropotkin" in Bol'shaia Sovetskaia Entsiklopedia, 2nd edition, 23 (Moscow, 1953), 485.
99. N. M. Pirumova, *Petr Alekseivich Kropotkin* (Moscow, 1972), pp. 46–47.
100. George Woodcock and Ivan Avakumovic, "The Anarchist Prince," *op. cit.*, p. 75.
101. Nicholas Walter (ed.), "Peter Kropotkin, Memoirs of a Revolutionist," *op. cit.*, p. 223.
102. *Ibid.*, p. 216.
103. *Ibid.*, pp. 216–17.
104. George Woodcock and Ivan Avakumovic, "The Anarchist Prince," *op. cit.*, pp. 76–77.
105. Nicholas Walter (ed.), "Peter Kropotkin, Memoirs of a Revolutionist," *op. cit.*, pp. 225, 227.
106. N. K. Lebedev, "P. A. Kropotkin," *op. cit.*, p. 30.
107. Martin A. Miller, "The Formative Years of P. A. Kropotkin, 1842–1876," *op. cit.*, pp. 206, 210.
108. N. K. Lebedev, "P. A. Kropotkin," *op. cit.*, pp. 31–33.
109. George Woodcock and Ivan Avakumovic, "The Anarchist Prince," *op. cit.*, p. 96.

110. Martin A. Miller, "The Formative Years of P. A. Kropotkin, 1842-1876," *op. cit.*, pp. 214-16.

111. George Woodcock and Ivan Avakumovic, "The Anarchist Prince," *op. cit.*, p. 106.

112. N. K. Lebedev, "P. A. Kropotkin," *op. cit.*, p. 34.

113. Martin A. Miller, "The Formative Years of P. A. Kropotkin, 1842-1876," *op. cit.*, p. 217

114. Nicolas Walter (ed.), "Peter Kropotkin, Memoirs of a Revolutionist," *op. cit.*, p. 287.

115. N. K. Lebedev, "P. A. Kropotkin," *op. cit.*, p. 36.

116. George Woodcock and Ivan Avakumovic, "The Anarchist Prince," *op. cit.*, p. 122.

117. Martin A. Miller, "The Formative Years of P. A. Kropotkin, 1842-1876," *op. cit.*, p. 230.

118. *Ibid.*, pp. 121-22.

119. Nicolas Walter (ed.), "Peter Kropotkin, Memoirs of a Revolutionist," *op. cit.*, pp. 304-305.

120. *Ibid.*, p. 306.

121. *Petr i Aleksandr Kropotkiny Perepiska*, II, 183-84.

122. Fernand Planche and Jean Delphy, *Kropotkine* (Paris, 1948), p. 53.

123. N. K. Lebedev, "P. A. Kropotkin," *op. cit.*, pp. 37-38.

124. George Woodcock and Ivan Avakumovic, "The Anarchist Prince," *op. cit.*, pp. 317-18.

125. Martin A. Miller, "The Formative Years of P. A. Kropotkin, 1842-1876," *op. cit.*, p. 258.

126. N. M. Pirumova, "Petr Alekseivich Kropotkin," *op. cit.*, pp. 67-68.

127. Martin A. Miller, "The Formative Years of P. A. Kropotkin, 1842-1876," *op. cit.*, pp. 271-73.

128. *Ibid.*, pp. 293-94, 301-302.

129. *Ibid.*, p. 305.

130. *Ibid.*, pp. 285-88.

131. George Woodcock and Ivan Avakumovic, "The Anarchist Prince," *op. cit.*, p. 131.

132. Martin A. Miller, "The Formative Years of P. A. Kropotkin, 1842-1876," *op. cit.*, p. 294.

133. Nicolas Walter (ed.), "Peter Kropotkin, Memoirs of a Revolutionist," *op. cit.*, p. 330.

134. N. K. Lebedev, "P. A. Kropotkin," *op. cit.*, pp. 40-42.

135. George Woodcock and Ivan Avakumovic, "The Anarchist Prince," *op. cit.*, p. 135.

136. Martin A. Miller, "The Formative Years of P. A. Kropotkin, 1842-1876," *op. cit.*, pp. 314-15, 319-22.

137. Nicolas Walter (ed.), "Peter Kropotkin, Memoirs of a Revolutionist," *op. cit.*, pp. 348-52, 377.

138. George Woodcock and Ivan Avakumovic, "The Anarchist Prince," *op. cit.*, p. 138.

139. Nicolas Walter (ed.), "Peter Kropotkin, Memoirs of a Revolutionist," *op. cit.*, pp. 378-79.

140. George Woodcock and Ivan Avakumovic, "The Anarchist Prince," *op. cit.*, p. 145.

141. Martin A. Miller, "The Formative Years of P. A. Kropotkin, 1842-1876," *op. cit.*, p. 369.

142. Nicolas Walter (ed.), "Peter Kropotkin, Memoirs of a Revolutionist," *op. cit.*, p. 381.

143. George Woodcock and Ivan Avakumovic, "The Anarchist Prince," *op. cit.*, pp. 150-52.

144. Martin A. Miller, "The Formative Years of P. A. Kropotkin, 1842-1876," *op. cit.*, p. 375.

145. N. M. Pirumova, "Petr Alekseivich Kropotkin," *op. cit.*, p. 102.

146. Nicolas Walter (ed.), "Peter Kropotkin, Memoirs of a Revolutionist," *op. cit.*, p. 417.

147. David Stafford, *From Anarchism to Reformism* (Toronto, Canada, 1971), pp. 64-66.

148. George Woodcock and Ivan Avakumovic, "The Anarchist Prince," *op. cit.*, pp. 175-77.

149. Nicolas Walter (ed.), "Peter Kropotkin, Memoirs of a Revolutionist," *op. cit.*, pp. 435-36.

150. *Ibid.*, p. 438.

151. *Ibid.*, pp. 451-52.

152. N. K. Lebedev, "P. A. Kropotkin," *op. cit.*, pp. 50-51.

153. *Ibid.*, p. 51.

154. Nicolas Walter (ed.), "Peter Kropotkin, Memoirs of a Revolutionist," *op. cit.*, p. 457.

155. *Ibid.*, p. 469.

156. George Woodcock and Ivan Avakumovic, "The Anarchist Prince," *op. cit.*, p. 212.

157. N. K. Lebedev, "P. A. Kropotkin," *op. cit.*, p. 52.

158. George Woodcock and Ivan Avakumovic, "The Anarchist Prince," *op. cit.*, p. 209.

159. *Ibid.*, pp. 225-29.

160. N. K. Lebedev, "P. A. Kropotkin," *op. cit.*, p. 53.

161. Nicolas Walter (ed.), "Peter Kropotkin, Memoirs of a Revolutionist," *op. cit.*, pp. 497-98.

162. *Ibid.*, p. 499.

163. *Ibid.*, pp. 499-500.

164. George Woodcock and Ivan Avakumovic, "The Anarchist Prince," *op. cit.*, p. 229.

165. N. K. Lebedev, "P. A. Kropotkin," *op. cit.*, p. 57.

166. George Woodcock and Ivan Avakumovic, "The Anarchist Prince," *op. cit.*, pp. 243-45.

167. N. K. Lebedev, "P. A. Kropotkin," *op. cit.*, pp. 59-60.

168. George Woodcock and Ivan Avakumovic, "The Anarchist Prince," *op. cit.*, pp. 274-82.

169. Peter Kropotkin, *Ideals and Realities in Russian Literature* (Westport, Connecticut, 1970), pp. 164, 168-69.

170. N. K. Lebedev, "P. A. Kropotkin," *op. cit.*, p. 61.

171. George Woodcock and Ivan Avakumovic, "The Anarchist Prince," *op. cit.*, pp. 61, 293-94.

172. *Ibid.*, p. 262.

173. Prince Kropotkin, *Ethics—Origin and Development* (New York, 1947), pp. ix-xiv.

174. George Woodcock and Ivan Avakumovic, "The Anarchist Prince," *op. cit.*, pp. 289, 296.

175. *Ibid.*, p. 297.

176. M. Korn, "P. A. Kropotkin i Russkoe Revolutsionnoe Dvizhenie," in G. P. Maksimov (ed.), *Internatsionalnyi Sbornik Posviashchennyi Desiatoi Godovshchine Smerti P. A. Kropotkina*, pp. 182-83.

177. Martin A. Miller, "The Formative Years of P. A. Kropotkin...," *op. cit.*, p. 379.

178. N. M. Pirumova, "Petr Alekseivich Kropotkin," *op. cit.*, pp. 103-104.

179. Martin A. Miller, *Kropotkin* (Chicago and London, 1976), p. 174.

180. George Woodcock and Ivan Avakumovic, "The Anarchist Prince," *op. cit.*, p. 357.

181. M. Korn, "P. A. Kropotkin i Russkoe Revolutsionnoe Dvizhenie," *op. cit.*, pp. 186-87.

182. Fernand Planche and Jean Delphy, *Kropotkine*, p. 122.

183. N. M. Pirumova, "Petr Alekseivich Kropotkin," *op. cit.*, pp. 169-71.

184. M. Korn, "P. A. Kropotkin i Russkoe Revolutsionnoe Dvizhenie," *op. cit.*, p. 189.

185. George Woodcock and Ivan Avakumovic, "The Anarchist Prince," *op. cit.*, pp. 363-64.

186. N. K. Lebedev, "P. A. Kropotkin," *op. cit.*, p. 62.

187. *Ibid.*, pp. 63-64.

188. N. Kareev, "P. A. Kropotkin O Velikoi Frantsuzskoi Revolutsii," in A. Borovoi and N. Lebedev (eds.), *Sbornik Statei Posviashchennyi Pamiati P. A. Kropotkina*, p. 117.

189. V. D. Bonch-Bruevich, Izbrannye Sochineniia, III, *Vospominaniia O V. I. Lenine, 1917-1924* (Moscow, 1963), p. 405.

190. N. M. Pirumova, "Petr Alekseivich Kropotkin," *op. cit.*, p. 173.

191. *Ibid.*, p. 175.

192. *Ibid.*, p. 179.

193. Prince Kropotkin, *The Terror in Russia* (London, 1909), p. 1.

194. *Ibid.*, pp. 2–7.
195. *Ibid.*, p. 29.
196. *Ibid.*, pp. 70–71.
197. *Ibid.*, p. 75.
198. N. K. Lebedev, "P. A. Kropotkin," *op. cit.*, pp. 65–66.
199. *Ibid.*, pp. 68–69.
200. George Woodcock and Ivan Avakumovic, "The Anarchist Prince," *op. cit.*, p. 380.
201. N. M. Pirumova, "Petr Alekseivich Kropotkin," *op. cit.*, p. 188.
202. George Woodcock and Ivan Avakumovic, "The Anarchist Prince," *op. cit.*, p. 382.
203. Fernand Planche and Jean Delphy, *Kropotkine*, p. 138.
204. George Woodcock and Ivan Avakumovic, "The Anarchist Prince," *op. cit.*, pp. 383–84.
205. M. Perro, "P. A. Kropotkin i Voina," in G. P. Maksimov (ed.), *Internatsionalnyi Sbornik . . .*, 163.
206. G. Sandomirsky, "Kropotkin i Frantsiia," in A. Borovoi and N. Lebedev (eds.), *Sbornik Statei et al.*, pp. 171, 173–74.
207. George Woodcock and Ivan Avakumovic, "The Anarchist Prince," *op. cit.*, pp. 388–91.
208. Martin A. Miller, "Kropotkin," *op. cit.*, p. 235.
209. N. K. Lebedev, "P. A. Kropotkin," *op. cit.*, pp. 72–73.
210 M. N. Pirumova, "Petr Alekseivich Kropotkin," *op. cit.*, p. 191.
211. N. K. Lebedev, "P. A. Kropotkin," *op. cit.*, p. 73.
212. David Shub, "Kropotkin and Lenin," *The Russian Review*, 12 (October 1953), 230.
213. Martin A. Miller, "Kropotkin," *op. cit.*, p. 236.
214. M. N. Pirumova. "Petr Alekseivich Kropotkin," *op. cit.*, pp. 193,
215. George Woodcock and Ivan Avakumovic," The Anarchist Prince," *op. cit.*, p. 408.
216. Voline, *The Unknown Revolution* (New York, 1975), p. 557.
217. N. K. Lebedev, "P. A. Kropotkin," *op. cit.*, p. 75.
218. David Shub, "Kropotkin and Lenin," *op. cit.*, p. 231.
219. N. M. Pirumova, "Petr Alekseivich Kropotkin," *op. cit.*, pp. 200–201.
220. Emma Goldman, *Living My Life*, II, 770–71.
221. *Ibid.*, p. 864.
222. V. D. Bonch-Bruevich, "Izbrannye Sochineniia," III, *op. cit.*, p. 406.
223. David Shub, "Kropotkin and Lenin," *op. cit.*, pp. 231–32.
224. Fernand Planche and Jean Delphy, *Kropotkine*, p. 162.
225. Paul Avrich (ed.), "The Anarchists in the Russian Revolution," *op. cit.*, p. 147.
226. *Ibid.*, pp. 148–49.
227. *Ibid.*, pp. 150–52.

228. George Woodcock and Ivan Avakumovic, "The Anarchist Prince," *op. cit.,* p. 437.

229. "Pismo De-Reigeru, December 23, 1920," in G. P. Maximov (ed.) *Internatsionalny Sbornik et al.,* pp. 200-201.

230. N. M. Pirumova, "Petr Alekseivich Kropotkin," *op. cit.,* p. 214.

231. Emma Goldman, *Living My Life,* II, 872.

232. George Woodcock and Ivan Avakumovic "The Anarchist Prince," *op. cit.,* p. 437.

233. Fernand Planche and Jean Delphy, *Kropotkine,* p. 171.

234. "Petr A. Kropotkin" in *Bol'shaia Sovetskaia Entsiklopedia,* Vol. 22, 2nd edition (Moscow, 1953), p. 485.

235. William Z. Foster, *History of the Three Internationals* (New York, 1968), p. 114.

Chapter Two

1. Peter A. Kropotkin, "Anarchism," *Encyclopaedia Britannica* (Eleventh Edition: New York, 1910) I, 914.

2. George Woodcock, *Anarchism—A History of Libertarian Ideas and Movements* (New York: World Publishing Co., 1971), pp. 10-11.

3. Herbert Read, *The Philosophy of Anarchism* (London: Freedom Press, 1940), p. 6.

4. Howard Zinn's "Introduction" in Herbert Read, *Anarchy and Order* (Boston, 1971), pp. ix-x.

5. Paul Berman (ed.), *Quotations from the Anarchists* (New York, 1972), p. 3.

6. *Ibid.,* p. 5.

7. Robert Hoffman (ed.), *Anarchism* (New York, 1970), p. 4.

8. George Woodcock "Anarchism" et al., *op. cit.,* pp. 23-24.

9. David Apter and James Joll (eds.), *Anarchism Today* (Garden City, N.Y., 1972), p. 3.

10. Daniel Guerin, *Anarchism* (New York and London, 1970), p. xii.

11. Irving L. Horowitz's "Introduction" to Irving L. Horowitz (ed.), *The Anarchists* (New York, 1964), p. 23.

12. *Ibid.,* pp. 17-18.

13. *Ibid.,* p. 22.

14. Leonard I. Krimerman and Lewis Perry, "Anarchism: The Method of Individualization," in Leonard I. Krimerman and Lewis Perry (eds.), *Patterns of Anarchy* (Garden City, N.Y., 1966), p. 557.

15. Marshall Shatz, "Introduction" in Marshal Shats (ed.), *The Essential Works of Anarchism* (New York, 1971), pp. xviii-xix.

16. George Woodcock, "Anarchism et al.," *op. cit.,* p. 27.

17. *Ibid.,* pp. 29-30.

18. Paul Berman (ed.) "Quotations from the Anarchists," *op. cit.,* p. 4.

19. Leonard I. Krimerman and Lewis Perry (eds.), "Patterns of Anarchy," *op. cit.*, p. 559.

20. George Woodcock, "Anarchism et al.," *op. cit.*, p. 34.

21. Paul Berman, "Introduction" in Paul Berman (ed.), "Quotations from the Anarchists," *op. cit.*, pp. 8-9.

22. *Ibid.*, p. 9.

23. *Ibid.*, p. 10.

24. Isaac Kramnick (ed.), *William Godwin, Enquiry Concerning Political Justice* (London, 1976), p. 76.

25. *Ibid.*, pp. 716-18.

26. Paul Eltzbacher, *Anarchism* (New York, 1960), p. 29.

27. Atendranath Bose, *A History of Anarchism* (Calcutta, India, 1967), pp. 85-87.

28. *Ibid.*, p. 89.

29. *Ibid.*, p. 97.

30. Isaac Kramnick, "Introduction," in Isaac Kramnick (ed.), *William Godwin, Enquiry Concerning Political Justice*, p. 21.

31. Irving L. Horowitz (ed.), *The Anarchists*, pp. 30-31.

32. *Ibid.*, 107.

33. April Carter *The Political Theory of Anarchism* (London, 1971), p. 17.

34. *Ibid.*, p. 25.

35. George Woodcock, "Anarchism et al.," *op. cit.*, pp. 84-85.

36. George Woodcock, *Pierre-Joseph Proudhon* (New York, 1972), pp. 272-73.

37. Marshal Shatz (ed.), *The Essential Works of Anarchism*, p. 81.

38. Martin Buber, *Paths in Utopia* (Boston, 1958), p. 28.

39. Atendranath Bose, *A History of Anarchism*, pp. 122-23.

40. Martin Buber, *Paths in Utopia*, pp. 33-34.

41. Stewart Edwards (ed.) *Selected Writings of P. -J. Proudhon* (Garden City, N.Y., 1969), pp. 26-27.

42. *Ibid.*, pp. 32-34.

43. P. -J. Proudhon, *What Is Property?* (New York, 1970), pp. 82-83.

44. George Woodcock, Anarchism et al., *op. cit.*, p. 114.

45. *P. -J. Proudhon, What Is Property?* p. 424.

46. Atendranath Bose, *A History of Anarchism* pp. 120, 122.

47. *Ibid.*, pp. 123-24

48. Stewart Edwards (ed.), *Selected Writings of P. -J. Proudhon*, pp. 56-61.

49. April Carter, *The Political Theory of Anarchism*, p. 64.

50. Paul Eltzbacher, *Anarchism*, pp. 55-57.

51. George Woodcock, "Anarchism et al.," *op. cit.*, pp. 120-21.

52. *Ibid.*, pp. 135, 140-41.

53. Irving L. Horowitz (ed.), *The Anarchists*, pp. 48-49.
54. Atendranath Bose, *A History of Anarchism*, pp. 158-59.
55. Max Stirner, *The Ego and His Own* (New York, 1973), p. 164.
56. Atendranath Bose, *A History of Anarchism*, pp. 164-66.
57. George Woodcock, "Anarchism et al.," *op. cit.*, p. 95.
58. Max Stirner, *The Ego and His Own*, p. 179.
59. George Woodcock, *Anarchism*, pp. 101-103.
60. Paul Eltzbacher, *Anarchism*, p. 75.
61. Paul Avrich, *The Russian Anarchists* (Princeton, N. J., 1967), p. 36.
62. Martin Malia, *Alexander Herzen and the Birth of Russian Socialism* (New York, 1965), pp. 400-403.
63. *Ibid.*, pp. 404-405.
64. *Ibid.*, pp. 408-409.
65. *Ibid.*, pp. 412-13.
66. *Ibid.*, p. 423.
67. *Ibid.*, pp. 417-18.
68. See Bert F. Hoselitz, "Preface," in G. P. Maximoff (ed.), *The Political Philosophy of Bakunin* (New York, 1953), p. 13.
69. George Woodcock, *Anarchism*, p. 147.
70. Marshall S. Shatz (ed.), *The Essential Works of Anarchism*, p. 124.
71. Bertrand Russell, *Roads to Freedom* (London and New York, 1965), pp. 46-48.
72. Irving L. Horowitz, *The Anarchists*, p. 38.
73. *Ibid.*, pp. 37-39.
74. E. H. Carr, *Michael Bakunin* (New York, 1961, p. 452 and p. 455.
75. Arthur Lehning (ed.), *Michael Bakunin, Selected Writings* (New York, 1974), pp. 136-37.
76. *Ibid.*, pp. 146-47.
77. Michael Bakunin, *God and the State* (Freeport, N.Y., 1971), pp. 30, 35.
78. Arthur Lehning (ed.), *Michael Bakunin, Selected Writings*, p. 149.
79. *Ibid.*, p. 167.
80. *Ibid.*, pp. 169-70.
81. *Ibid.*, p. 172.
82. *Ibid.*
83. *Ibid.*, p. 173.
84. *Ibid.*, pp. 26-27.
85. *Ibid.*, p. 240.
86. *Ibid.*, pp. 254-55.
87. *Ibid.*, p. 266.

88. *Ibid.*, pp. 268-69.
89. Eugene Pyziur, *The Doctrine of Anarchism of Michael A. Bakunin* (Chicago, 1955), p. 130.
90. Sam Dolgoff, "Introduction," in Sam Dolgoff (ed.), *Bakunin on Anarchy* (New York, 1971) p. 10.
91. Arthur Lehning (ed.), *Michael Bakunin, Selected Writings,* pp. 68-69.
92. *Ibid.*, pp. 71-74
93. *Ibid.*, pp. 76-78.
94. *Ibid.*, p. 82.
95. *Ibid.*, pp. 82-83.

Chapter Three

1. Peter Kropotkin, *Mutual Aid* (New York, 1972), pp. 30-32.
2. *Ibid.*, pp. 35-36, 44-49, 54.
3. *Ibid.*, pp. 68-69.
4. *Ibid.*, p. 81.
5. *Ibid.*, p. 122.
6. *Ibid.*, pp. 163-65.
7. *Ibid.*, p. 245.
8. Peter Kropotkin, *Ethics—Origin and Development* (New York, 1947), p. 15.
9. *Ibid.*, pp. 16-17.
10. *Ibid.*, p. 300.
11. *Ibid.*, p. 2.
12. Pierre Kropotkine, *Paroles d'un Révolté* (Paris, 1896), pp. 3-8.
13. *Ibid.*, p. 13.
14. *Ibid.*, p. 25.
15. Peter Kropotkin, "Expropriation," in Martin A. Miller (ed.), *P. A. Kropotkin, Selected Writings on Anarchism and Revolution,* p. 176.
16. Pierre Kropotkine, *Paroles d'un Révolté, op. cit.,* pp. 29-31.
17. *Ibid.*, p. 41.
18. *Ibid.*, pp. 88-89.
19. *Ibid.*, pp. 147-54.
20. *Ibid.*, pp. 159-61.
21. *Ibid.*, pp. 270-72.
22. *Ibid.*, pp. 312-313.
23. *Ibid.*, p. 314.
24. P. A. Kropotkin, "Revolutionary Studies," *Commonweal* (1892), p. 6.
25. *Ibid.*, pp. 9-10.
26. *Ibid.*, pp. 16-18.
27. *Ibid.*, pp. 28-30.

28. Peter Kropotkin, *The Great French Revolution* (New York, 1927), I, pp. 2–3.

29. *Ibid.*, p. 3.

30. *Ibid.*, pp. 95–96.

31. *Ibid.*, p. 97.

32. *Ibid.*, p. 184.

33. *Ibid.*, pp. 497–98.

34. *Ibid.*, pp. 533, 537.

35. *Ibid.*, III, p. 575.

36. P. Kropotkin, "Must We Occupy Ourselves with an Examination of the Ideal of a Future System?" in Martin A. Miller (ed.), *Selected Writings on Anarchism and Revolution*, pp. 82–83.

37. *Ibid.*, p. 287.

38. P. Kropotkin, " Revolutionary Government," Roger Baldwin (ed.), *Kropotkin's Revolutionary Pamphlets*, pp. 248–49.

39. P. Kropotkin, "Expropriation," in Martin A. Miller (ed.) *Selected Writings on Anarchism and Revolution*, pp. 168, 173.

40. *Ibid.*, p. 182.

41. *Ibid.*, p. 183.

42. *Ibid.*, pp. 184–85.

43. *Ibid.*, pp. 194–96.

44. *Ibid.*, pp. 202–03.

45. *Ibid.*, pp. 205–206.

46. Peter Kropotkin, *Ideals and Realities in Russian Literature* (Westport, Conn., 1970), pp. 298–99.

47. P. Kropotkin, "Anarchist Communism: Its Basis and Principles," in Roger Baldwin (ed.), *Kropotkin's), Kropotkin's Revolutionary Pamphlets*, p. 46.

48. *Ibid.*, p. 52.

49. *Ibid.*, p. 53.

50. Pierre Kropotkin, *The Place of Anarchism in Socialistic Evolution* (London, 1887), p. 6.

51. *Ibid.*, pp. 11–12.

52. Peter Kropotkin, *The Conquest of Bread* (New York, 1972), p. 94.

53. *Ibid.*, pp. 15–16.

54. Peter Kropotkin, "The State: Its Historic Role," in Martin A. Miller (ed.), *Selected Writings on Anarchism and Revolution*, pp. 233–36.

55. *Ibid.*, p. 264.

56. Peter Kropotkin, "Modern Science and Anarchism," in Roger Baldwin (ed.), *Kropotkin's Revolutionary Pamphlets*, pp. 176–80.

57. *Ibid.*, pp. 181–84.

58. Peter Kropotkin, "Anarchism: Its Philosophy and Ideal," in Roger Baldwin (ed.), *op cit.*, pp. 139–40.

59. Peter Kropotkin, "Law and Authority," in Roger Baldwin (ed.), *ibid.,* p. 203.

60. *Ibid.,* p. 218.

61. Peter Kropotkin, "Anarchist Morality," in Roger Baldwin (ed.), *ibid.,* pp. 98-99.

62. *Ibid.,* pp. 108-109.

63. Peter Kropotkin, *The Conquest of Bread* (New York, 1972), pp. 44-46.

64. *Ibid.,* pp. 49-50.

65. *Ibid.,* pp. 51-53.

66. Peter Kropotkin, *The Conquest of Bread,* p. 132.

67. Pierre Kropotkin, *War* (London, n.d.), Second Edition, p. 4.

68. Peter Kropotkin, *The Conquest of Bread,* p. 122.

69. *Ibid.,* pp. 125-27.

70. *Ibid.,* p. 140.

71. *Ibid.,* p. 174.

72. *Ibid.,* pp. 183-86.

73. Peter Kropotkin, *Fields, Factories and Workshops,* (Boston and N.Y., 1899), pp. 5-6.

74. *Ibid.,* pp. 47-48.

75. *Ibid.,* p. 103.

76. *Ibid.,* pp. 149-50.

77. *Ibid.,* pp. 171-72.

78. *Ibid.,* pp. 206-10.

79. *Ibid.,* pp. 221-23.

80. *Ibid.,* pp. 226-27.

81. *Ibid.,* pp. 229-31.

82. *Ibid.,* p. 233.

83. *Ibid.,* p. 258.

84. *Ibid.,* p. 259.

85. *Ibid.,* pp. 261-63.

86. *Ibid.,* pp. 274-75.

87. Peter Kropotkin, *In Russian and French Prisons* (New York, 1971), pp. 25-26.

88. *Ibid.,* p. 309.

89. *Ibid.,* p. 315.

90. *Ibid.,* pp. 323-24.

91. *Ibid.,* p. 331.

92. *Ibid.,* pp. 333-34.

93. Peter Kropotkin, "Prisons and Their Moral Influence on Prisoners," Roger Baldwin (ed.), *Kropotkin's Revolutionary Pamphlets,* p. 223.

94. Peter Kropotkin, *In Russian and French Prisons,* pp. 365-66.

95. *Ibid.,* pp. 367-68.

96. *Ibid.,* pp. 370-71.

Chapter Four

1. Bob Galois, "Ideology and the Idea of Nature: The Case of Peter Kropotkin," *Antipode*, 8 (Sept. 1976), 5.

2. *Ibid.*, p. 5.

3. *Ibid.*, pp. 6-7

4. *Ibid.*, p. 7.

5. *Ibid.*, p. 8

6. *Ibid.*, pp. 9-10

7. *Ibid.*, pp. 11-13

8. I. Grossman-Roshchin, "Mysli O Tvorchestve P. A. Kropotkina," in Aleksei Borovoi and Nikolai Lebedev (eds.), *Sbornik Statei Posviaschennyi Pamiati P. A. Kropotkina*, p. 14.

9. *Ibid.*, p. 15.

10. *Ibid.*, p. 19.

11. *Ibid.*, p. 21.

12. *Ibid.*, p. 22.

13. Aleksei Borovoi, "Problema Lichnosti v Uchenii P. A. Kropotkina," in Aleksei Borovoi and Nikolai Lebedev (eds.), *Sbornik Statei et al.*, pp. 32-33.

14. De Roberti, *Petr Kropotkin-Lichnost i Doktrina*, (St. Petersburg, 1906), p. 22.

15. Aleksei Borovoi, "Problema Lichnosti v Uchenii P. A. Kropotkina," *op. cit.*, pp. 47-48.

16. Peter Kropotkin, *Mutual Aid* (Boston, n.d.), p. 166.

17. *Ibid.*, pp. 171-72.

18. *Ibid.*, p. 182.

19. *Ibid.*, pp. 215-21.

20. Peter Kropotkin, "The State: Its Historic Role," in Martin A. Miller (ed.), *Selected Writings on Anarchism and Revolution—P. A. Kropotkin*, p. 231.

21. *Ibid.*, p. 235.

22. Marc Bloch, *Feudal Society* (Chicago, 1974) II, p. 355.

23. Doris Mary Stenton, *English Society in the Early Middle Ages* (London, 1955), pp. 178-79.

24. Peter Kropotkin, *The Conquest of Bread* (New York, 1972), pp. 146-47.

25. Thomas Masaryk, *The Spirit of Russia* (London, 1961) II, 380.

26. Alexander Gray, *The Socialist Tradition* (London, 1946), pp. 366-67.

27. Vernon Richards (ed,), *Errico Malatesta, His Life and Ideas* (London, 1965), p. 261.

28. Derry Novak, "The Place of Anarchism in the History of Political Thought," in Robert Hoffman (ed.), *Anarchism*, p. 24.

29. Rudolf Roker, "Petr Kropotkin i Ego Tvorchestvo," in G. P.

Maksimov (ed.), *International'nyi Sbornik Posviashchennyi Desiatoi Godovshchine Smert: P. A. Kropotkina,* pp. 14-15.

30. *Ibid.,* p. 16.
31. *Ibid.,* p. 24.
32. Martin A. Miller, *Kropotkin* (Chicago, 1976), pp. 180-82.
33. *Ibid.,* pp. 25-26.
34. *Ibid.,* pp. 26-27.
35. P. Arshinov, "Formy i Printsipy Organizatsii Anarkhistov v Bor'ba Za Kommunizm i Anarkhizm," in G. P. Maksimov (ed.), *Internatsional'nyi Sbornik et al.,* pp. 169-73.
36. Anthony D'Agostino, *Marxism and the Russian Anarchists* (San Francisco, 1977), pp. 237-43.
37. Camillo Berneri, *Peter Kropotkin—His Federalist Ideas* (London, 1942), p. 5.
38. *Ibid.,* p. 22.
39. Vincent C. Punzo, "The Modern State and the Search for Community: The Anarchist Critique of Peter Kropotkin," *International Philosophical Quarterly,* XVII (March 1976), 5.
40. *Ibid.,* pp. 7-8
41. *Ibid.,* p. 10.
42. *Ibid.,* p. 12.
43. *Ibid.,* p. 30.
44. *Ibid.,* p. 32.
45. Emile Capouya and Keitha Tompkins (eds.), *The Essential Kropotkin* (New York, 1975), pp. xv-xvi.
46. Frank Pierce, *Crimes of the Powerful* (London, 1976), p. 20.
47. *Ibid.,* p. 66.
48. Martin Buber, *Paths in Utopia* (Boston, 1971), p. 43.
49. *Ibid.,* pp. 44-45.
50. *Ibid.,* p. 46.
51. Richard Sennett, *The Uses of Disorder* (New York, 1971), pp. 108, 157-58.
52. *Ibid.,* p. 179.
53. *Ibid.,* p. 183.
54. *Ibid.,* p. 174.
55. John Hewetson, *Mutual Aid and Social Evolution* (London, 1946), pp. 22-23
56. George Bernard Shaw, *The Impossibilities of Anarchism,* (London, 1893), pp. 102-103.
57. Bertrand Russell, *Roads to Freedom (London and New York* 1965), pp. 74-77.
58. *Ibid.,* pp. 82-83.
59. *Ibid.,* p. 96.
60. April Carter, *The Political Theory of Anarchism* (London, 1971), pp. 78, 86.

61. Roel van Duyn, *Message of a Wise Kabouter* (London, 1972), pp. 56-58.

62. Barrington Moore, Jr., *Reflections on the Causes of Human Misery* (Boston, 1973), pp. 72-75.

63. Aileen Kelly, "Lessons of Kropotkin," *New York Review of Books* (October 28, 1976), pp. 41-42.

64. "Kropotkin" in *Bol'shaia Sovetskaia Entsiklopedia,* 3rd Edition (Moscow, 1973), 13, 481.

65. F. Ia. Polianskii, *Sotsializm i Sovremennyi Anarkhizm* (Moscow, 1973), pp. 28-29.

66. Vernon Richards (ed.), *Errico Malatesta, His Life and Ideas,* p. 265.

67. Colin Ward, "Introduction" to Colin Ward (ed.), *Peter Kropotkin, Fields, Factories and Workshops Tomorrow* (N.Y., Evanston, San Francisco, London, 1975), p. 13.

68. Emile Capouya and Keitha Tompkins, "Introduction" in Emile Capouya and Keitha Tompkins (eds.), *The Essential Kropotkin,* pp. viii-xix.

69. G. D. H. Cole, *A History of Socialist Thought* (New York, 1964) II, pp. 348-49.

70. Max Nettlau, *Ocherki Po Istorii Anarkhicheskikh Idei i Stati Po Razym Sot'sialnym Voprosam* (Detroit, 1951), pp. 129-30.

71. Joseph Stalin, *Anarchism or Socialism?* (New York, 1953), pp. 32-32.

72. F. Ia. Polianskii, *Kritika Ekonomicheskikh Teorii Anarkhizma* (Moscow, 1976), p. 195.

73. *Ibid.,* p. 212, pp. 242-43.

74. *Ibid.,* pp. 249-50.

75. *Ibid.,* pp. 283-84.

76. *Ibid.,* p. 295.

77. *Ibid.,* p. 301.

78. *Ibid.,* p. 180.

79. *Ibid.,* pp. 218-20.

80. Catharinus D. van Dusseldorf, "Peter Kropotkin-Grepen Uit Denken En Werken Van Een Idealist," unpublished Doctoral Dissertation, (Amsterdam, Holland, n.d.), pp. 79-81.

81. M. Tugan-Baranovsky, *Modern Socialism in Its Historical Development* (New York, 1966), p. 179.

82. Radoslav Selucky, "Marxism and Self-Management," *Critique No. 3* (Autumn 1974), pp. 59-60.

83. H. H. Ticktin, "Socialism, the Market, and the State. Another View: Socialism vs. Proudhonism," *Critique No. 3* (Autumn 1974), pp. 68-71.

84. Charles Bettelheim, *Calcul Economique et Formes de Propriete* (Paris, 1970), p. 36.

85. *Ibid.*, p. 122.

86. Aurel Friedmann, "Das Anarcho-Kommunistische System das Fursten Peter Kropotkin," unpublished Doctoral Dissertation, The University of Cologne (Köln, Germany, 1931), p. 14.

87. George Gaylord Simpson, *The Meaning of Evolution* (New York, 1957), pp. 155-63.

88. C. H. Waddington, *The Ethical Animal* (Chicago, 1967), pp. 59, 149.

89. *Ibid.*, p. 162.

90. Niko Tinbergen, "On War and Peace in Animals and Man," in Gunter Altner (ed.), *The Human Creature* (Garden City, N.Y., 1974) pp. 235-37.

91. Theodosius Dobzhansky, *Genetic Diversity and Human Equality* (New York, 1973), pp. 27-38.

92. Rene Dubos, *So Human an Animal* (New York, 1968), pp. 85-98, 120.

93. W. C. Allee, *Cooperation Among Animals* (New York, 1951), revised, p. 12.

94. V. C. Wynne-Edwards, *Animal Dispersion in Relation to Social Behavior* (New York, 1962), p. 127; William Etkin (ed.), *Social Behavior and Organization among Vertebrates* (Chicago, 1964), p. 6; Peter Klopper and Jack Hailman, *An Introduction to Animal Behavior* (Englewood Cliffs, N. J., 1967), p. 139.

95. W. C. Allee, "Where Angels Fear to Tread: A Contribution from General Sociology to Human Ethics," *Science*, 97 (June 11, 1943), 518-25; W. C. Allee, *Cooperation Among Animals*, pp. 212-13.

96. Irenaus Eibl-Eibesfeldt, *Love and Hate* (New York, 1972), pp. 245-46; see also her *Ethology—The Biology of Behavior* (New York, 1975), 2nd Edition pp. 510, 533.

97. Robert L. Trivers, "The Evolution of Reciprocal Altruism," *The Quarterly Review of Biology*, 46 (March 1971), 48.

98. Garrett Hardin, *Nature and Man's Fate* (New York, 1961), pp. 219-20.

99. Garrett Hardin, *The Limits of Altruism* (Bloomington and London, 1977), pp. 26-27.

100. *Ibid.*, pp. 80-81, 97-98.

101. Konrad Lorenz, *On Aggression* (New York, 1971), pp. 39-48.

102. *Ibid.*, pp. 233-38.

103. Robert Ardrey, *African Genesis* (New York, 1961), pp. 31-32.

104. Robert Ardrey, *The Territorial Imperative* (New York, 1975), pp. 3-5, 73, 94-95.

105. Robert Ardrey, *The Social Contract* (New York, 1974), pp. 3, 37-41.

106. Desmond Morris, *The Naked Ape* (New York, 1976), pp. 20-21, 34, 121-22.

107. Lionel Tiger and Robin Fox, *The Imperial Animal* (New York, 1971), pp. 21-25.

108. *Ibid.*, pp. 33-37, 208-16.

109. Anthony Storr, *Human Aggression* (New York, 1970), p. 15.

110. *Ibid.*, pp. 58-59, 63-64.

111 Jerome Michael Carello, "Instinct, Learning and the New Social Darwinism," *The Modern Schoolman*, 54 (Jan. 1977), 142-44.

112. David P. Barash, *Sociobiology and Behavior* (New York, 1977), p. 226.

113. Robert J. Richards, "The Innate and the Learned: The Evolution of Konrad Lorenz's Theory of Instinct," *Philosophy of the Social Sciences*, IV (June-Sept. 1974), 116-26.

114. T. C. Schneirla, "Instinct and Aggression," in M. F. Ashley Montagu (ed.), *Man and Aggression* (London, Oxford, N.Y., 1968), p. 63.

115. John Hurrell Crook, "The Nature and Function of Territorial Aggression," in M. F. Ashley Montagu (ed.), *Man and Aggression*, pp. 151-53.

116. *Ibid.*, pp. 173-74.

117. John Paul Scott, *Aggression* (Chicago and London, 1975), 35, 63-64.

118. *Ibid.*, pp. 68-69.

119. Ashley Montagu, *The Nature of Human Aggression* (London and N.Y., 1976) p. 9, 21.

120. Ashley Montagu, *Darwin—Competition and Cooperation* (Westport, Conn., 1973), pp. 47-48, 53-56; see also his *Man in Process* (Cleveland and N.Y., 1961), pp. 57-58.

121. Ashley Montagu, *On Being Human* (New York, 1966), pp. 29-39.

122. Edward O. Wilson, *Sociobiology—The New Synthesis* (Cambridge, Mass., 1975), pp. 508-509, 550.

123. "Against Sociobiology," *New York Review of Books* (Nov. 13, 1975), pp. 43-44.

124. Joseph S. Alper, "Biological Determinism," *Telos*, No. 31 (Spring 1977), pp. 166-68.

125. *Ibid.*, p. 169.

126. See Alexander Alland, Jr., *The Human Imperative* (New York, 1972), pp. 20-24.

Chapter Five

1. Ruth Link-Salinger, *Gustav Landaver—Philosopher of Utopia* (Indianapolis, 1977), pp. 61-62.

2. Eugene Lunn, *Prophet of Community* (Berkeley, L.A., London, 1973), p. 104.

3. *Ibid.*, pp. 150-51.
4. *Ibid.*, pp. 172-76.
5. *Ibid.*, pp. 216-20.
6. Gustav Landaver, *For Socialism* (St. Louis, 1978), pp. 137-44.
7. *Ibid.*, pp. 9-12.
8. Richard Drinnon, "Introduction" in *Emma Goldman, Anarchism and Other Essays* (New York, 1969) p. xiii.
9. *Ibid.*, p. 43.
10. *Ibid.*, p. 52.
11. *Ibid.*, p. 54.
12. *Ibid.*, pp. 65-66.
13. *Ibid.*, pp. 73-78.
14. Paul Avrich, "Introduction" in Alexander Berkman, *What is Communist Anarchism?* (New York, 1972), p. xiii.
15. *Ibid.*, p. 69
16. *Ibid.*, p. 86.
17. *Ibid.*, p. 203.
18. *Ibid.*, p. 227.
19. *Ibid.*, p. 249.
20. *Ibid.*, pp. 272-74.
21. Herbert Read, *The Philosophy of Anarchism* (London, 1940), pp. 28-29.
22. Herbert Read, *Anarchy and Order* (Boston, 1971), pp. 17-18.
23. *Ibid.*, p. 105.
24. *Ibid.*, p. 133.
25. *Ibid.*, p. 132.
26. *Ibid.*, p. 134.
27. *Ibid.*, pp. 154-55.
28. *Ibid.*, pp. 212-14.
29. Murray Bookchin, *Post-Scarcity Anarchism* (Berkeley, California, 1971), p. 13.
30. *Ibid.*, pp. 93-95.
31. *Ibid.*, p. 136.
32. *Ibid.*, pp. 20-21.
33. *Ibid.*, pp. 41-43.
34. Murray Bookchin, "Radical Agriculture," in *Radical Agriculture* (New York, 1976), pp. 7-12.
35. Murray Bookchin, *Post-Scarcity Anarchism*, p. 43.
36. *Ibid.*, p. 69.
37. *Ibid.*, pp. 215-17.
38. Colin Ward, *Anarchy in Action* (New York, 1974), pp. 98-99.
39. *Ibid.*, pp. 99-101.
40. *Ibid.*, p. 107.
41. *Ibid.*

42. *Ibid.*, p. 140.

43. *Ibid.*, p. 142.

44. April Carter, *The Political Theory of Anarchism* (London, 1971), pp. 105, 109-10.

45. Lewis Mumford, *The Myth of the Machine*, Vol. I— *Technics and Human Development* (New York, 1967), p. 3.

46. *Ibid.*, pp. 3-4.

47. *Ibid.*, p. 7.

48. *Ibid.*, p. 9.

49. *Ibid.*, pp. 252-55.

50. *Ibid.*, p. 255.

51. *Ibid.*, Vol. II— *The Pentagon of Power*, p. 155.

52. *Ibid.*, p. 156.

53. Lewis Mumford, *The City in History* (New York, 1961), p. 514.

54. Paul Goodman, *People or Personnel and Like a Conquered Province* (New York, 1968), pp. 17-18.

55. *Ibid.*, p. 117.

56. *Ibid.*, pp. 119-21.

57. *Ibid.*, pp. 317-18.

58. *Ibid.*, pp. 326-27.

59. *Ibid.*, p. 332.

60. *Ibid.*, p. 334.

61. Richard Merrill's "Preface" in *Radical Agriculture* (New York, 1976), p. xvi.

62. *Ibid.*, p. xvii.

63. Sheldon L. Greene, "Corporate Accountability and the Family Farm," in *Radical Agriculture*, p. 53.

64. Michael Perelman, "Efficiency in Agriculture: The Economics of Energy," in *Radical Agriculture*, p. 65.

65. Peter Barnes, "Land Reform in America," in *Radical Agriculture*, p. 27.

66. Michael Perelman, "Efficiency in Agriculture," *op. cit.*, p. 67.

67. Wendell Berry, "Where Cities and Farms Come Together," *Radical Agriculture*, pp. 15-16.

68. *Ibid.*, pp. 16-20.

69. Darryl McLeod, "Urban-Rural Food Alliances: A Perspective on Recent Community Food Organization," *Radical Agriculture*, pp. 201, 203-204.

70. Alex Comfort, *The Nature of Human Nature* (New York, 1968), p. 220.

71. Alex Comfort, *Authority and Delinquency in the Modern State* (London, 1950), p. 109.

72. *Ibid.*, p. 102.

73. Alex Comfort, *The Nature of Human Nature*, p. 224.

74. *Ibid.*, p. 228.
75. Alex Comfort, *Sexual Behavior in Society* (New York, 1950), pp. 138–39.
76. Theodore Roszak, "Introduction", in E. F. Schumacher, *Small Is Beautiful* (New York, 1973), pp. 3–4.
77. E. F. Schumacher, *Small Is Beautiful*, pp. 17–20.
78. *Ibid.*, p. 28.
79. *Ibid.*, pp. 30–34.
80. *Ibid.*, p. 35.
81. *Ibid.*, pp. 40–41.
82. *Ibid.*, p. 42.
83. *Ibid.*, p. 47.
84. *Ibid.*, pp. 138–39.
85. *Ibid.*, p. 145.
86. *Ibid.*, pp. 250–51.
87. *Ibid.*, pp. 269–70.
88. *Ibid.*, pp. 272–73.

Selected Bibliography

PRIMARY SOURCES

1. Books

The Conquest of Bread. London, Chapman and Hall, 1906.

Dnevnik P. A. Kropotkina (Kropotkin's Diary). Moscow and Petrograd: Gos. Izdat, 1923.

Ethics: Origin and Development. New York: McVeagh, 1924.

Fields, Factories and Workshops. London: Hutchinson And Co., 1899.

The Great French Revolution. London: Heinemann, 1909.

Ideals and Realities in Russian Literature. New York: Alfred A. Knopf, 1915.

In Russian and French Prisons. London: Ward and Downey, 1887.

Memoirs of a Revolutionist. Boston: Houghton Mifflin, 1899.

Modern Science and Anarchism. Philadelphia: Social Science Club, 1903.

Mutual Aid. London: Heinemann, 1902.

Paroles d'un Revolté. Paris: 1885.

Perepiska Petra i Aleksandra Kropotkinyikh (Correspondence of Peter and Alexander Kropotkin). 2 volumes. Moscow and Leningrad: Academia, 1932–33.

The Terror in Russia. London: Methuen and Co., 1909.

2. Pamphlets and Articles

"Anarchism," *Encyclopaedia Britannica,* 11th Edition (1910).

Anarchism: Its Philosophy and Ideal. Freedom Pamphlets, No. 10. London, 1897.

Anarchist Communism: Its Basis and Principles. Freedom Pamphlets, No. 4. London, 1891.

Anarchist Morality. Freedom Pamphlets, No. 6. London, 1892.

An Appeal to the Young. London: Modern Press, 1885.

The Commune of Paris. London: Freedom Press, 1909.

"The Constitutional Agitation in Russia," *Nineteenth Century,* 57, No. 335 (January 1905).

Law and Authority. London: Freedom Press, 1886.

The Place of Anarchism in Social Evolution. London: W.
    Reeves, 1886.
"The Present Crisis in Russia," *North American Review,* 172
    (1901).
"Representative Government," *Commonweal,* 7, Nos. 312–21
    (1892).
"Revolutionary Government," *Commonweal,* 7, Nos. 325–27
    (1892).
"Revolutionary Studies," *Commonweal,* 7, Nos. 294–300
    (1891–1892).
The Wage System. Freedom Pamphlets, No. 1, London, 1889.
War. London: H. Seymour, 1886.

3. Anthologies of Kropotkin's Writings
BALDWIN, ROGER N., ed. *Kropotkin's Revolutionary Pamphlets.* New
    York: Vanguard Press, 1927.
CAPOUYA, EMILE, and TOMPKINS, KEITHA, eds. *The Essential Kropotkin.*
    New York: Liveright, 1975.
MILLER, MARTIN A., ed. *Selected Writings on Anarchism and Revolu-
    tion. P. A. Kropotkin.* Cambridge, Mass.: The M.I.T. Press, 1970.
READ, HERBERT, ed. *Kropotkin. Selections from his Writings.* London:
    Freedom Press, 1942.

SECONDARY SOURCES

1. Books, Booklets, and Theses Primarily about Kropotkin
BERNERI, CAMILLO. *Peter Kropotkin—His Federalist Ideas.* London:
    Freedom Press, 1942.
BOROVOI, ALEKSEI, and LEBEDEV, NIKOLAI, eds. *Sbornik Statei Posvi-
    ashchennyi Pamiati P. A. Kropotkina.* Petersburg-Moscow: Golos
    Truda, 1922.
DE ROBERTI. *Petr Kropotkin—Lichnost i Doktrina.* St. Petersburg:
    Iakor, 1906.
FRIEDMANN, AUREL. "Das Anarcho-Kommunistische System des Fürsten
    Peter Kropotkin." Ph.D. dissertation. University of Köln, 1931.
GROSSMAN-ROSHCHIN, I. *Kharakteristika Tvorchestva P. A. Kropotkina.*
    Petersburg-Moscow: Golos Truda, 1921.
HEWETSON, JOHN. *Mutual Aid and Social Evolution—Mutual Aid and
    the Social Significance of Darwinism.* London: Freedom Press,
    1946.
ISHILL, JOSEPH, ed. *Peter Kropotkin—The Rebel, Thinker and
    Humanitarian.* Berkeley Heights, New Jersey: Free Spirit Press,
    1923.
LEBEDEV, NIKOLAI. *P. A. Kropotkin.* Moscow: Gos. Izdat., 1925.

MAKSIMOV, G. P., ed. *Internatsional'nyi Sbornik Posviashchennyi Desiatoi Godovshchine Smerti P.A. Kropotkina.* Chicago: Knigoizdatelstva Federatsii Russkikh Anarcho-Kommunistiche.

MILLER, MARTIN A. *Kropotkin.* Chicago: The University of Chicago Press, 1976.

——. "The Formative Years of P. A. Kropotkin, 1842–1876: A Study of the Origins and Development of Populist Attitudes in Russia." Ph.D. dissertation, University of Chicago, 1967.

PIRUMOVA, H. M. *Petr Alekseivich Kropotkin.* Moscow: Izdat. Nauka, 1972.

PLANCHE, FERNAND, and DELPHY, JEAN. *Kropotkine.* Paris: Editions S.L.I.M., 1948.

VAN DUSSELDORF, CATHERINUS DROSSAANT. "Grepen Uit Denken En Werken Van Een Idealist." Ph.D. dissertation. Amsterdam, n.d.

VAN DUYN, ROEL. *Message of a Wise Kabouter.* London: Duckworth, 1972.

WOODCOCK, GEORGE, and AVAKUMOVIC, IVAN. *The Anarchist Prince.* London and New York: T. V. Boardman, 1950.

2. Articles Primarily about Kropotkin

GALOIS, BOB. "Ideology and the Idea of Nature: The Case of Peter Kropotkin." *Antipode* (September 1976), pp. 1–16.

KELLY, AILEEN. "Lessons of Kropotkin." *New York Review of Books* (October 28, 1976), pp. 40–44.

PUNZO, VINCENT C. "The Modern State and the Search for Community: The Anarchist Critique of Peter Kropotkin." *International Philosophical Quarterly,* XVI (March 1976), 3–32.

SHUB, DAVID. "Kropotkin and Lenin." *The Russian Review,* XII (October 1953), 227–34.

3. Books Relating to Kropotkin and His Ideas or to Anarchism

ALLAND, ALEXANDER. *The Human Imperative.* New York: Columbia University Press, 1972.

ALLEE, W. C. *Cooperation Among Animals.* New York: Henry Schuman, 1951.

APTER, DAVID E., and JOLL, JAMES, eds. *Anarchism Today.* Garden City, New York: Anchor Books, 1972.

ARDREY, ROBERT. *African Genesis.* New York: Dell Publishing Co., 1967.

——. *The Hunting Hypothesis.* New York: Atheneum Publishers, 1976.

——. *The Social Contract.* New York: Dell Publishing Co., 1974.

——. *The Territorial Imperative.* New York: Dell Publishing Co., 1971.

AVRICH, PAUL, ed. *The Anarchists in the Russian Revolution.* Ithaca, New York: Cornell University Press, 1973.
AVRICH, PAUL. *The Russian Anarchists.* Princeton: Princeton University Press, 1967.
BERKMAN, ALEXANDER. *What Is Communist Anarchism?* New York: Dover Publications, 1972.
BERMAN, PAUL, ed. *Quotations from the Anarchists.* New York: Praeger Publishers, 1972.
BOOKCHIN, MURRAY. *Post-Scarcity Anarchism.* Berkeley, California: Ramparts Press, 1971.
BUBER, MARTIN *Paths in Utopia.* Boston: Beacon Press, 1971.
CARTER, APRIL. *The Political Theory of Anarchism.* London: Routledge and Kegan Paul, 1971.
COLE, G. D. H. *History of Socialist Thought.* Vol. II. Marxism and Anarchism 1850-1890. London: Macmillan & Co., 1964.
D'AGOSTINO, ANTHONY. *Marxism and the Russian Anarchists.* San Francisco: Germina Press, 1977.
DOBZHANSKY, THEODOSIUS. *Genetic Diversity and Human Equality.* New York: Basic Books, Inc., 1973.
DUBOS, RENE. *So Human an Animal.* New York: Charles Scribners, 1968.
EIBL-EIBESFELDT, IRENÄUS. *Ethology—The Biology of Behavior.* New York: Holt Rinehart and Winston, 1975.
———. *Love and Hate.* New York: Holt, Rinehart and Winston, 1972.
FORMAN, JAMES D. *Anarchism.* New York: Dell Publishing Co., 1975.
GOLDMAN, EMMA. *Anarchism and Other Essays.* New York Dover Publications, 1969.
———. *Living My Life,* Vol. I and Vol. II. New York: Dover Publications, 1970.
———. *My Disillusionment in Russia.* London: C.W. Daniel Co., 1925.
GOODMAN, PAUL. *People or Personnel and Like a Conquered Province.* New York: Vintage Books, 1968.
GRAY, ALEXANDER. *The Socialist Tradition.* London: Longmans, Green and Co., 1946.
GUERIN, DANIEL. *Anarchism.* New York: Monthly Review Press, 1970.
HARDIN, GARRETT. *The Limits of Altruism.* Bloomington & London: Indiana University Press, 1977.
HARDIN, GARRETT. *Nature and Man's Fate.* New York: Mentor Books, 1961.
HARE, RICHARD. *Portraits of Russian Personalities between Reform and Revolution.* London: Oxford University Press, 1959.
HOFFMAN, ROBERT, ed. *Anarchism.* New York: Lieber-Atherton, 1973.
HOROWITZ, IRVING L., ed. *The Anarchists.* New York: Dell Publishing Co., 1964.
HULSE, JAMES W. *Revolutionists in London.* London: Clarenden Press, 1970.

JOLL, JAMES. *The Anarchists.* Boston: Little, Brown and Co., 1964.

KILROY-SILK, ROBERT. *Socialism Since Marx.* New York: Taplinger, 1972.

KRIMERMAN LEONARD I., and PERRY, LEWIS, eds. *Patterns of Anarchy.* Garden City, N.Y.: Anchor Books, 1966.

LORENZ, KONRAD. *On Aggression.* New York: Bantam Books, 1971.

MONTAGU, ASHLEY. *Darwin—Competition and Cooperation.* Westport, Connecticut: Greenwood Press, 1973.

———., ed. *Man and Aggression.* London, Oxford, N.Y.: Oxford University Press, 1968.

———. *Man In Process.* Cleveland and New York: The World Publishing Co., 1961.

———. *The Nature of Human Aggression.* New York: Oxford University Press, 1976.

———. *On Being Human.* New York: Hawthorn Books, Inc., 1966.

MORRIS, DESMOND. *The Human Zoo.* New York: Dell Publishing Co., 1971.

———. *The Naked Ape.* New York: Dell Publishing Co., 1976.

MUMFORD, LEWIS. *The City In History.* New York: Harcourt Brace and World, 1961.

———. *The Pentagon of Power.* New York: Harcourt Brace Jovanovich, 1970.

———. *Technics and Human Development.* New York: Harcourt Brace Jovanovich, 1967.

NISBET, ROBERT. *The Social Philosophers—Community and Conflict in Western Thought.* New York: Thomas Y. Crowell Co., 1973.

POLIANSKII, F. Ia. *Kritika Ekonomicheskikh Teorii Anarkhizma.* Moscow: Izdutel'stvo Moskovskogo Universiteta, 1976.

———. *Sotsializm i Sovremennyi Anarkhizm.* Moscow: Izdutel'stvo "Ekonomika," 1973.

READ, HERBERT. *Anarchy and Order.* Boston: Beacon Press, 1971.

RICHARDS, VERNON, ed. *Errico Malatesta, His Life and Ideas.* London: Freedom Press, 1965.

RUNKLE, GERALD. *Anarchism Old and New.* New York: Delacorte Press, 1972.

SCHUMACHER, E. F. *Small Is Beautiful—Economics as if People Mattered.* New York: Harper and Row, 1973.

SCOTT, JOHN PAUL. *Aggression.* Second Edition Revised and Expanded. Chicago and London: The University of Chicago Press, 1975.

SHATZ, MARSHALL S., ed. *The Essential Works of Anarchism.* New York: Bantam Books, 1971.

SIMPSON, GEORGE GAYLORD. *Biology and Man.* New York: Harcourt Brace Jovanovich, 1968.

STORR, ANTHONY. *Human Aggression.* New York: Bantam Books, 1970.

TIGER, LIONEL, and FOX, ROBIN. *The Imperial Animal.* New York: Delta Books, 1971.

TUGAN-BARANOVSKY, D. M. *Modern Socialism in Its Historical Development.* New York: Russell and Russell, 1966.
WADDINGTON, C. H. *The Ethical Animal.* Chicago: University of Chicago Press, 1967.
WARD, COLIN. *Anarchy in Action.* New York: Harper and Row, 1974.
WILSON, EDWARD O. *Sociobiology—The New Synthesis.* Cambridge, Massachusetts: Harvard University Press, 1975.
WOODCOCK, GEORGE. *Anarchism—A History of Libertarian Ideas and Movements.* New York: World Publishing Co., 1971.

4. Articles Concerned with Kropotkinian Ideas and Issues

ALLEE, W.C. "Where Angels Fear to Tread: A Contribution from General Sociology to Human Ethics." *Science,* 97 (June 11, 1943), 517-25.
ERIKSON, ERIK H. "Psychoanalysis and Ongoing History: Problems of Identity, Hatred and Nonviolence. " *The American Journal of Psychiatry,* 122 (Sept. 1965), 241-50.
FOWLER, R. B. "The Anarchist Tradition of Political Thought" *Western Political Quarterly,* XXV (Dec. 1972), 738-52.
HOFSTADTER, RICHARD. "Discussion" (following Erikson article above). *The American Journal of Psychiatry,* 122 (Sept. 1965), 250-53.

Index